Targets of the Global Goals

Targets of the Global Goals

Dominic Billings

Dom Billings

To Roz, with love and gratitude for your support.

Introduction	1
Goal #1	5
Target 1.1	6
Target 1.2	8
Target 1.3	10
Target 1.4	12
Target 1.5	14
Target 1.A	16
Target 1.B	18
Goal #2	19
Target 2.1	20
Target 2.2	22
Target 2.3	24
Target 2.4	25
Target 2.5	27
Target 2.A	27
Target 2.B	30
Target 2.C	32
Goal #3	33
Target 3.1	34
Target 3.2	36
Target 3.3	38
Target 3.4	41
Target 3.5	42
Target 3.6	44
Target 3.7	45
Target 3.8	47
Target 3.9	49
Target 3.A	51
Target 3.B	52
Target 3.C	54
Target 3.D	55
Goal #4	57

Target 4.1	58
Target 4.2	60
Target 4.3	61
Target 4.4	62
Target 4.5	63
Target 4.6	64
Target 4.7	65
Target 4.A	67
Target 4.B	68
Target 4.C	69
Goal #5	70
Target 5.1	71
Target 5.2	73
Target 5.3	75
Target 5.4	77
Target 5.5	78
Target 5.6	79
Target 5.A	81
Target 5.B	82
Target 5.C	83
Goal #6	84
Target 6.1	85
Target 6.2	86
Target 6.3	87
Target 6.4	88
Target 6.5	90
Target 6.6	91
Target 6.A	92
Target 6.B	93
Goal #7	94
Target 7.1	95
Target 7.2	96
Target 7.3	97
Target 7.A	98

Target 7.B	99
Goal #8	100
Target 8.1	101
Target 8.2	102
Target 8.3	103
Target 8.4	104
Target 8.5	106
Target 8.6	107
Target 8.7	108
Target 8.8	110
Target 8.9	112
Target 8.10	113
Target 8.A	114
Target 8.B	115
Goal #9	116
Target 9.1	117
Target 9.2	118
Target 9.3	120
Target 9.4	121
Target 9.5	122
Target 9.A	123
Target 9.B	124
Target 9.C	125
Goal #10	126
Target 10.1	127
Target 10.2	128
Target 10.3	129
Target 10.4	130
Target 10.5	131
Target 10.6	132
Target 10.7	134
Target 10.A	136
Target 10.B	137
Target 10.C	138

- Goal #11 — 139
  - Target 11.1 — 140
  - Target 11.2 — 142
  - Target 11.3 — 143
  - Target 11.4 — 144
  - Target 11.5 — 145
  - Target 11.6 — 147
  - Target 11.7 — 148
  - Target 11.A — 149
  - Target 11.B — 150
  - Target 11.C — 151
- Goal #12 — 152
  - Target 12.1 — 153
  - Target 12.2 — 154
  - Target 12.3 — 155
  - Target 12.4 — 156
  - Target 12.5 — 158
  - Target 12.6 — 159
  - Target 12.7 — 160
  - Target 12.8 — 161
  - Target 12.A — 162
  - Target 12.B — 163
  - Target 12.C — 164
- Goal #13 — 165
  - Target 13.1 — 166
  - Target 13.2 — 167
  - Target 13.3 — 169
  - Target 13.A — 170
  - Target 13.B — 171
- Goal #14 — 172
  - Target 14.1 — 173
  - Target 14.2 — 174
  - Target 14.3 — 175
  - Target 14.4 — 176

Target 14.5	177
Target 14.6	178
Target 14.7	179
Target 14.A	180
Target 14.B	181
Target 14.C	182
Goal #15	183
Target 15.1	184
Target 15.2	186
Target 15.3	188
Target 15.4	189
Target 15.5	190
Target 15.6	192
Target 15.7	193
Target 15.8	194
Target 15.9	195
Target 15.A	196
Target 15.B	197
Target 15.C	198
Goal #16	199
Target 16.1	200
Target 16.2	201
Target 16.3	203
Target 16.4	204
Target 16.5	205
Target 16.6	206
Target 16.7	207
Target 16.8	209
Target 16.9	210
Target 16.10	211
Target 16.A	212
Target 16.B	213
Goal #17	214
Target 17.1	215

Target 17.2	216
Target 17.3	217
Target 17.4	218
Target 17.5	219
Target 17.6	220
Target 17.7	220
Target 17.8	222
Target 17.9	223
Target 17.10	224
Target 17.11	225
Target 17.12	226
Target 17.13	227
Target 17.14	228
Target 17.15	229
Target 17.16	230
Target 17.17	231
Target 17.18	232
Target 17.19	233
References	234

Introduction

The time of publication of this book might seem peculiar, given there's five years left until the designated due date of 2030 for the Global Goals. Barring a miracle, the world won't achieve most or all Goals.

The 2024 Sustainable Development Report deemed 16% progress so far across all Goals worldwide.[1] At the time of writing, the Pact for the Future, adopted at the UN Summit of the Future, has given the first sign the UN may extend the Goals beyond 2030. In likelihood, this will be through to mid-century for some Goals and Targets, 2040 for others, and others sticking to the original 2030 deadline.

These 17 Goals, based upon the precepts of the concept of sustainable development, are the guiding agenda through to 2030 for the UN, adopted by all 193 of its Member States by unanimity in 2015.

The UN Open Working Group (OWG) developed the Targets and Goals in 2013-14, bringing together Member States, UN agencies, NGOs, scientists, and civil society groups to discuss and negotiate.

The deliberations of the Open Working Group, across 13 sessions, resulted in a proposed 169 Targets. Reaching consensus on these Targets came from a deliberative process via many amendments, additions and deletions, distilled to the 169 Targets which were adopted. The official UN Indicators, of which there are now 231, took much longer, until March 2017 - well after the adoption of the SDGs in September 2015, with several refinements since.

The structure of Goals, targets and indicators, was set as a precedent by the Millennium Development Goals (MDGs), which preceded the SDGs from 2000-2015, and of which the SDGs build upon, with 8 MDGs, 21 targets, and 60 indicators.

Goals are often empty if not meeting the SMART criteria of specific, measurable, achievable, relevant and time-bound. The SDGs and Targets are time-bound by the 2015-2030 period, though several Targets have end dates of 2020 or other time periods. The Goals and Targets are measurable by 231 official UN Indicators. Some Targets aren't specific in their wording, for example, setting the aim to "increase", without specifying how much, whereas others are clearer e.g. "end hunger," or "double agricultural productivity." For many targets lacking in specificity, their Indicators quantify this better, although there are examples of Indicators which don't appear to have direct relevance to the text of its Target.

The title of this book could be Targets and Indicators of the Global Goals. Like any aspirational and ambitious goals, it's helpful and important to break them up - in this instance, from Goals to Targets beneath them, and below these, measurable Indicators.

This book will introduce readers who may not already be familiar with many of the various bodies and agencies which make up the UN. Whatever opinion you may bring toward the UN, it's a forum for each country to gather on equal footing to establish consensus, and the many UN treaties mentioned in this book have the power of international law. When signed and ratified by a country, these treaties become supreme to the country's domestic law. The UN Charter is the "world constitution," supreme to any law anywhere on the face of the planet. Its opening stanza is "We the peoples of the United Nations..." The United Nations is for everyone - not just Member States and their heads of state and government, but you, the individual.

We're all citizens of a country, and as each country of the world adopted the SDGs, the 2030 Agenda - which is the formal document by which all UN Member States adopted the SDGs - is the agenda for all 8 billion of us and rising.

The country of which you're a citizen, and represents you on the world stage at the UN, adopted these Goals on your behalf. They're a reflection of unanimity across the borders of 193 countries – such a consensus is an astonishing feat.

Should we not meet the Sustainable Development Goals, the planet will still turn. But we'll likely miss the window of time by which our species, and our fellow furry and feathered brethren, rotate on the face of it.

To avert this, we only need to make a handful of adjustments, which by comparison to the stakes, aren't onerous.

The primary one is the transfer of money from those who have it in surplus, to the needy. We do this, so they can see the end of tomorrow without dying of preventable starvation or disease.

Though there's been a meagre 16% progress on the Goals so far, this hasn't been because the adopted Goals were over-ambitious. The solutions have been available - what's been absent is the political will, and most important, the finance. The budget to achieve the SDGs is only a couple trillion dollars more than current levels, which sounds like a lot, but not so, considering this is 1-2% of a gross world product of $100 trillion.[2]

Most countries can afford this from their own national budgets, should they wish to prioritise it. The exceptions are the 1.5 billion people living in the 59 least developed countries, which need external aid - a budgeted $400 billion per year until 2030 - again, a small sum compared to the gross world product. This $400 billion financing gap for the least developed countries to achieve the SDGs is equal to 0.7% of the economies of the high-income countries, which have been committing this exact proportion as aid since 1970, but they continue to deny.

The second major change shares with the first the need to change our mind. We need to accept we have been carrying on with life a certain way, which while we may not have realised it, it was detrimental. It's regrettable, but hard to flail yourself for what you haven't known.

But this dynamic shifts once you realise your behaviour, until now, has been of detriment to others. What follows from coming into this newfound knowledge, or revelation one's past actions were misdeeds, can lead to a seizing up. You might not know how to set forth. But enough time passes, and this tension within us must resolve itself. Your mind – and morality – will shift, and your outlook and behaviour alike.

We need the world population to undergo the dynamic, as described above, to get to where we want to achieve the Global Goals. It's not an easy task for one's psyche to reconcile, nor communicating the needed changes to the masses. We need time which we don't have to allow our behaviours to follow suit after coming into our new learnings.

This book doesn't prescribe how to achieve the Sustainable Development Goals. It specifies what we need to do, and expands on how we'll measure it. My first book on the topic of the SDGs, entitled *You and the Global Goals* addresses how to achieve the Goals at the individual level.

For expert resources on addressing how to achieve the SDGs, I recommend the body of work of the Sustainable Development Solutions Network (SDSN), an initiative of UN Secretary General Ban Ki-Moon, alongside President of the SDSN, Professor Jeffrey Sachs.

This book isn't a psychological how-to for the needed skills to manage grappling with 169 Targets and more than 200 Indicators below these. Remembering and aligning 169 of anything is a lot to coordinate, and 17 Goals was already too many.

But this is life and death for billions of people – born, and still to be - and what seems like an infinite number of other individual lifeforms.

If you've completed an upper secondary education, you can handle this. It might strain your brain, but this is a small price to pay in the face of what we're staring down the barrel of.

It's implausible the agenda of Global Goals isn't inspiring, and could be anything but a reflection of a universal expression of our shared morals.

We all have a part to play, and can sit on the sidelines. But there is an alternative. We need action, requiring energy, which we may be reluctant to expend if we're feeling uncertain. This is why we need to familiarise ourselves with the Targets of the Global Goals. Because our strongest organ is always our brains. The only exertion needed is your attention, and your eyes to move across a page. Your brain will process the rest, and action can follow once you've come into this knowledge and allowed it to digest.

You can help to achieve these Goals, but it's necessary to familiarise ourselves at a more thorough level with 169 further sub-topics beyond the 17 broader Goals, and how to measure our efforts by 231 official UN Indicators.

Lastly, the Our World in Data team has collated, and presented as graphs, much of the forthcoming data. Our World in Data is an amazing initiative offering open access data and visualisations under Creative Commons BY. A handful of visualisations have cropped footnotes from the original. My thanks to the Our World in Data team for providing the clearest presentation available of SDG progress via its SDG Tracker project.

Goal #1

End poverty in all its forms everywhere

Target 1.1

By 2030 eradicate extreme poverty for all people everywhere, currently measured as people living on less than $1.25 a day.

To measure Target 1.1, there is one Indicator:

- Indicator 1.1.1: Proportion of the population living below the international poverty line by sex, age, employment status and geographic location (urban/rural)

The ambitious aim of Target 1.1 is eradicating extreme poverty for all people everywhere. The year 2030 has been set as the deadline for the world to meet in alignment with the Sustainable Development Goals as a whole.

The World Bank's definition of extreme poverty is based on an international poverty line. The World Bank is an international financial institution within the UN system, which provides loans to developing countries, with the aim of poverty eradication. The World Bank measured the international poverty line, as living on less than $US1.25 a day. Since the 193 UN Member States adopted the SDGs, the World Bank has raised the measure of extreme poverty to $1.90, and then again to $2.15. Though wherever one may live, and whatever the local prices of goods and services, $2 a day is scarcely enough to meet basic needs.

More than 700 million people met the definition of living in extreme poverty when the UN Member States adopted the SDGs in 2015, the overwhelming majority living in Sub-Saharan Africa and South Asia.[3]

Before the industrial era, beginning in the middle of the 19th century, close to the whole human population lived in a state of extreme poverty, but since the turn of the millennium, there's been a steady decrease.

One of the key reasons for this encouraging drop in extreme poverty rates was the power of the Millennium Development Goals (MDGs), the preceding development framework of the UN before the adoption of the SDGs. The focus of the MDGs was on the fight against extreme poverty, and its accompanying ills, with the SDGs building upon these efforts.

The sister goal of SDG #1 was MDG #1, which was to halve extreme poverty levels by 2015, using the international poverty line measure of $1.25 of income, from a baseline of 1990 levels. The world met Millennium Development Goal #1 five years before its due date, in 2010, in large part due to the astounding growth rates of China in the MDG period between 2000 and 2015. MDG #1 saw a billion people lifted from extreme poverty, compared to 1990, when half the population of developing countries lived under $1.25 a day, though leaving behind 700 million people at the end of the MDG period in 2015.

According to the World Data Lab, as of December 2024, 615,558,000 people live in extreme poverty.[4] At this date, a rate of 0.5 people per second were falling into extreme poverty, yet the targeted rate for escaping extreme poverty by 2030 was 3 people per second - the world off-track by 303,066,000 people. This trend projects 7% of the global population, or 599 million people, would still be living in extreme poverty by 2030, missing Target 1.1.

The COVID-19 pandemic affected progress on this Goal and Target, with the global extreme poverty rate rising in 2020 for the first time in over 20 years, though there were signs of slowing progress even before this, compounded by conflict and climate change.

Target 1.2

By 2030, reduce at least by half the proportion of men, women and children of all ages living in poverty in all its dimensions according to national definitions.

To measure Target 1.2, there are two Indicators:

- Indicator 1.2.1: Proportion of population living below the national poverty line, by sex and age
- Indicator 1.2.2: Proportion of men, women and children of all ages living in poverty in all its dimensions according to national definitions

Defining poverty "according to national definitions" contrasts with the international definition of extreme poverty, and instead relates to 'relative poverty,' which depends on the cost of living in different countries. Each country has its own poverty line - the threshold for its individual citizens or households to meet basic needs.

Another measure of poverty used is consumption expenditure equal to $US3.20 a day, including food bought and produced by the household. In 2015, 1.9 billion people, or 26% of the global population, lived on less than $3.20 a day, reduced by only 1%, or 140 million, by 2020, though down from more than half the global population in 1990.[5] The number of people living under $3.20 a day in 2020 was comparable to the amount living on $1.90 a day in 1990. Half of those living under $3.20 a day in 2020 lived in South Asia, as did a quarter of the extreme poor. Sub-Saharan Africa was home to two-thirds of the world's population living in extreme poverty, and a third under the $3.20 poverty line. East Asia has seen huge progress on eradicating extreme poverty in the past three decades, but as of 2018, 150 million East Asians lived under the $3.20 poverty line.

Another factor of importance in achieving this goal, not reflected in the UN's official Indicators, is total fertility rate, with more births per woman leading to population growth, a trend forecast for those countries still mired in extreme poverty, eroding sustainable development efforts. As well as a reflection of living in poverty, high fertility rates are often related to poor access to reproductive health options.

A global aggregate share of populations living below national poverty lines isn't available to see if it's on track to halve by 2030, per the aims of Target 1.2. For the countries with highest shares living below their respective national poverty lines, most have insufficient data to observe any trends of a halving of poverty according to national definition.[6]

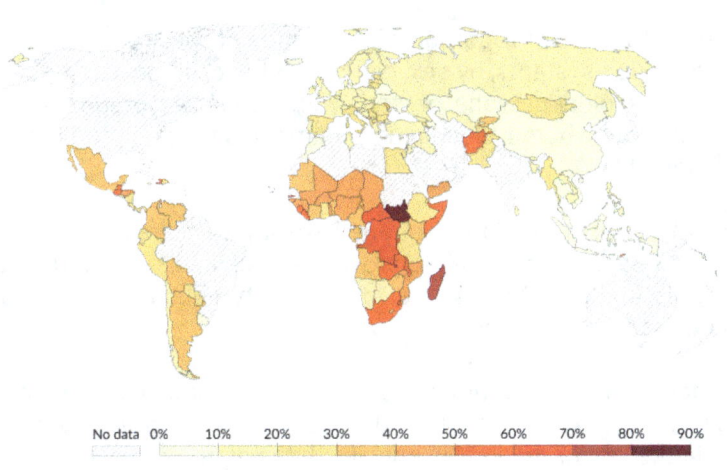

Target 1.3

Implement nationally appropriate social protection systems and measures for all, including floors, and by 2030 achieve substantial coverage of the poor and the vulnerable.

To measure Target 1.3, there is one Indicator:

- Indicator, 1.3.1: Proportion of population covered by social protection systems, by sex, distinguishing children, unemployed persons, older persons, persons with disabilities, pregnant women, newborns, work-injury victims and the poor and the vulnerable.

The 'floor' of social protection mentioned in Target 1.3 are human rights which aim to guarantee services to provide a threshold, for a lifetime of the essentials, including health care, food security, education, housing, and other goods and services.

Social protections are government-sponsored programs designed to shield the vulnerable. To promote and protect citizens, governments intervene in the labour market via social safety net programs e.g. Medicare and Medicaid in the US, Social Security, unemployment benefits. Social protections are common to European countries who pioneered the model, which have a tradition of taxing and transferring to provide for the social safety net.

Not all countries can raise enough tax revenue for their population to protect the vulnerable with social protections. If the average citizen lives on a bare subsistence, enough to survive hand-to-mouth, day-to-day, they don't have a surplus of income beyond survival for the government to tax. The government thus has a meagre tax base to collect from, with which to provide services to improve wellbeing.

In other instances, there may be less of an appetite from the government or electorate to raise enough taxes to support such transfers, due to societal stigmas toward certain vulnerable groups. There may be enough surplus income to provide for a potential tax base, but taxpayers may have a resistance to government revenue being transferred to others as welfare.

These gaps are what Target 1.3 aims to remedy by 2030. As of 2020, only 47% of the global population were covered by at least one social protection benefit, the remainder exposed to economic shocks in the market for wage labour which could impact their quality of life.[7]

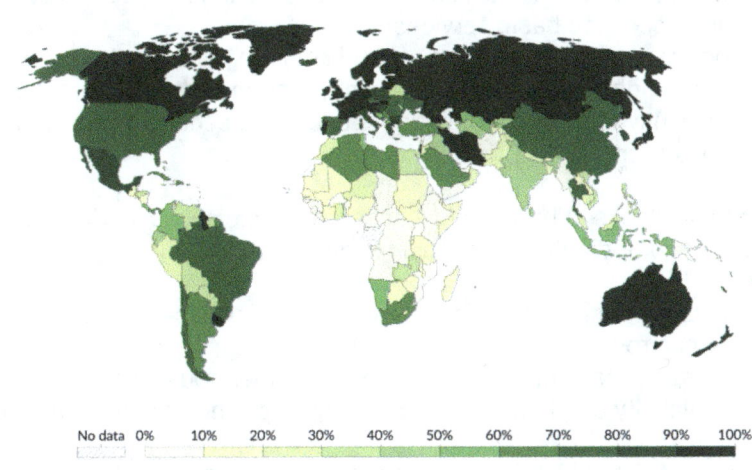

Target 1.4

By 2030, ensure that all men and women, in particular the poor and the vulnerable, have equal rights to economic resources, as well as access to basic services, ownership and control over land and other forms of property, inheritance, natural resources, appropriate new technology and financial services, including microfinance.

- Indicator 1.4.1: Proportion of population living in households with access to basic services
- Indicator 1.4.2: Proportion of total adult population with secure tenure rights to land, (a) with legally recognized documentation, and (b) who perceive their rights to land as secure, by sex and type of tenure.

Indicator 1.4.1 looks at households' access to basic services. Under the UN definition for Indicator 1.4.1, basic services are:

- government provision of drinking water services within a 30-minute round trip
- sanitation facilities not shared with another household
- availability of a handwashing facility on premises with soap and water
- clean fuels, which don't contribute to unhealthy indoor air quality
- convenient access to transport
- waste collection
- basic health care and education
- broadband internet access

Also mentioned in Target 1.4 is microfinance, the provision of banking and lending facilities to individuals or small businesses, in a way they otherwise wouldn't be able to access due to their low levels of income.

Indicator 1.4.2 looks at what proportion of adults in each country's population have secure tenant rights to the occupation and ownership of land, including the passing on of property between generations of families. Indicator 1.4.2 is disaggregated by sex, recognising the prevalence of inequality for women in matters of tenure and inheritance laws. Indicator 1.4.2 also disaggregates by types of tenure, an example being a leasehold, by which a lessee contracts with a lessor to use the property for payments over the period of the lease. Another type of tenure is customary, according to the customs of Indigenous communities. The other two tenure types are public tenure i.e. property owned by the state, and freehold, which is owning the property, its land, and the space above it. Tenure systems face challenges due to global stresses on food security and urbanisation, and there's now greater demand for land reforms in favour of the poor. There are two necessary concepts to meet the definition of secure tenant rights for the purposes of Indicator 1.4.2: legal documentation, and an individual's feeling of the security of their tenure. An example of the latter is a fear of involuntary loss of land due to a disagreement over land rights, irrespective of such tenure's official recognition.

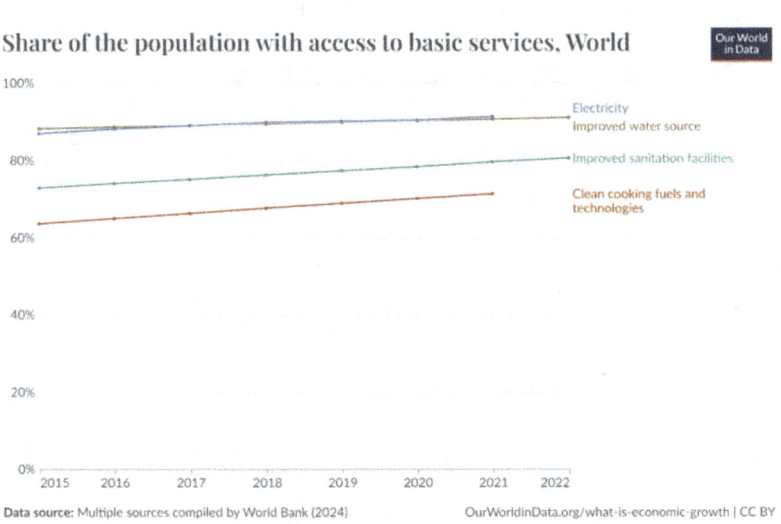

Target 1.5

By 2030, build the resilience of the poor and those in vulnerable situations and reduce their exposure and vulnerability to climate-related extreme events and other economic, social and environmental shocks and disasters.

- Indicator 1.5.1: Number of deaths, missing persons and persons affected by disaster per 100,000 people.
- Indicator 1.5.2: Direct disaster economic loss in relation to global gross domestic product (GDP).
- Indicator 1.5.3: Number of countries that adopt and implement national disaster risk reduction strategies in line with the Sendai Framework for Disaster Risk Reduction 2015–2030.
- Indicator 1.5.4: Proportion of local governments that adopt and implement local disaster risk reduction strategies in line with national disaster risk reduction strategies.

Target 1.5 acknowledges disasters in developing countries cause 95% of global deaths from disasters, and visit loss and damage 20 times greater upon developing countries, as a percentage of GDP.[8]

Indicator 1.5.1 measures:

- the number of people who died during, afterward, or as a direct result of a hazardous event
- those whose whereabouts are unknown since
- those who suffered injury or illness

- the number of people evacuated, displaced, or suffered direct damage to their livelihoods and assets

Indicator 1.5.2 measures economic loss attributed to a disaster, whether direct or indirect, inclusive of homes, hospitals, schools, physical infrastructure, industrial plants, crops, and livestock.

Indicator 1.5.3 focuses on a global policy relevant to all Indicators of Target 1.5. All UN Member States adopted the Sendai Framework for Disaster Risk Reduction 2015-2030 in 2015. The Sendai Framework pertains to worldwide goals responding to disaster risk reduction, adopted at a conference hosted in Sendai, the largest city in Japan's north-eastern Tohoku region, which was the epicentre of the catastrophic 2011 earthquake and tsunami.

Indicator 1.5.4 measures the percentage of local governments who've adopted and implemented disaster risk reduction strategies.

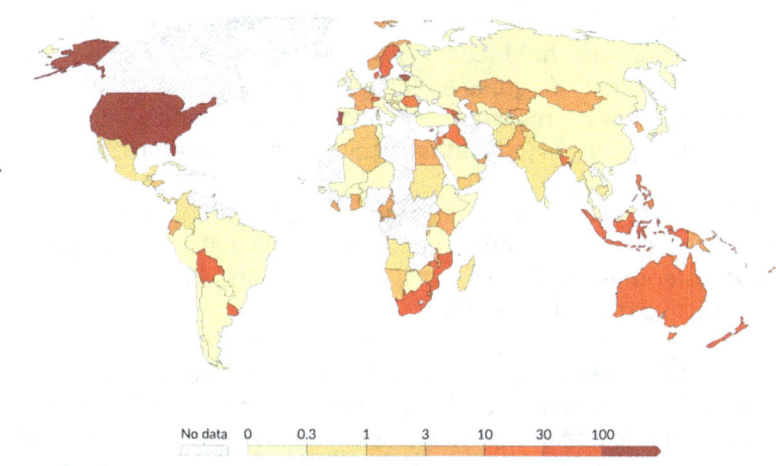

Target 1.A

Ensure significant mobilization of resources from a variety of sources, including through enhanced development cooperation, in order to provide adequate and predictable means for developing countries, in particular least developed countries, to implement programmes and policies to end poverty in all its dimensions.

- Indicator 1.a.1: Total official development assistance grants from all donors that focus on poverty reduction as a share of the recipient country's gross national income.
- Indicator 1.a.2: Proportion of total government spending on essential services (education, health, and social protection).

Target 1.a is the first example of a Target named by letters, rather than the earlier Targets' designation by numbers. For all the SDGs, Targets measuring outcomes are designated by numbers, and Targets with letters are means of implementation.

Indicator 1.a.1 focuses upon the concept of official development assistance (ODA). The aim of ODA is to improve the economic and social development of humans living in developing countries. The degree to which a country is 'developing' is often defined by a country's score in the Human Development Index (HDI), a composite measure of life expectancy, years of education, and per capita income. Separate, though entwined, to ODA, is humanitarian aid, which is more synonymous with logistical help in the face of disaster or conflict. ODA is a concept defined in 1969 by the Organisation of Economic Cooperation and Development (OECD), an international organisation of 38 member states, with a focus on economic policies. 30 of these OECD members constitute the largest aid donors, which form a committee to discuss poverty reduction efforts. The predominant means of measuring ODA is as a percentage of the donor country's gross national income (GNI), which is similar to the concept of GDP (gross domestic product), but by contrast, GNI includes the economic output of foreign residents of the country.

The OECD has an official List of ODA Recipients, all the developing countries and territories eligible to receive ODA. To count as ODA, donor flows must come from government agencies, and the aim must be for the economic development and welfare of developing countries. The aid must be concessional too i.e. grants with no obligation to be repaid, or loans with much more generous repayment terms than are available in the market.

The sectors counted toward poverty reduction for the purposes of Indicator 1.a.1 include food aid, basic health, education, water and sanitation, population programmes and reproductive health.

In 2023, the 30 high-income country donors spent only 0.37% of their collective gross national income in aid toward basic needs, far below the 0.7% of GNI committed by these countries across decades, though reneged upon.[9] The only exceptions among these 30 countries to meet or exceed the 0.7% commitment were Denmark, Sweden, Norway, Luxembourg and Germany.

Indicator 1.a.2 is the total spending on education, health, and social protection, from all levels of government, as a percentage of government expenditure. The rationale of Indicator 1.a.2 is public expenditure reflects the priority given to each government's focus on improving wellbeing.

Relevant to Indicator 1.a.2 is UNESCO's recommendation of 15-20% public expenditure on education. But as of 2021, the world had spent a total of 12% of all government expenditure on education, and 12% for health.

Target 1.B

Create sound policy frameworks at the national, regional and international levels, based on pro-poor and gender-sensitive development strategies, to support accelerated investment in poverty eradication actions.

- Indicator 1.b.1: Pro-poor public social spending

'Pro-poor' is a term in the jargon of development studies for policies targeting the poor and poverty reduction. 'Gender-sensitivity' is a term surrounding efforts to create awareness around gender, as gender roles affect our behaviours, and changing them, if necessary, engenders a better sense of equality.

Indicator 1.b.1 is the share of government expenditure on health, education, and cash transfers for the direct benefit of those living in poverty.

At the time of writing, there's no data available for this indicator.

Goal #2

End hunger, achieve food security and improved nutrition and promote sustainable agriculture

Target 2.1

By 2030, end hunger and ensure access by all people, in particular the poor and people in vulnerable situations, including infants, to safe, nutritious and sufficient food all year round.

- Indicator 2.1.1: Prevalence of undernourishment.
- Indicator 2.1.2: Prevalence of moderate or severe food insecurity in the population, based on the Food Insecurity Experience Scale

SDG #2 flowing on from SDG #1 implies the obvious interrelationship between poverty and hunger. Target 2.1 of the SDGs corresponds to Target 1.C of the MDGs, which was to "Halve, between 1990 and 2015, the proportion of people who suffer from hunger." The world met Target 1.C of the MDGs, but still left 795 million people undernourished, including 90 million children under the age of 5.[10]

The aim, by 2030, is to achieve zero hunger as part of SDG #2. As of 2022, 9% of the global population, equal to 735 million, continued to experience hunger and undernourishment.[11] One of the UN agencies focused on alleviating hunger and ensuring food security is the Food and Agriculture Organisation (FAO). The FAO identified the total number of those living in a state of hunger has risen about 1% since 2015 - the main culprits being COVID, climate, conflict, and recessions.

The definition of undernourishment is a diet with insufficient nutrients to provide the energy for a healthy and active life. At the most extreme, tragic end of undernourishment, is starvation. We're familiar with the heart-rending images of children displaying the hallmarks of malnutrition. The medical term, marasmus, is often characterised by the wasted mass of emaciation from energy deficiency. The cause of distended abdomens is from a swelling of fluid retention, and a liver overwhelmed with fatty deposits. The condition, termed kwashiorkor, is from having enough calories, but deficient in protein, which can occur when children are no longer nursing from breast milk and have moved to a diet of starchy carbohydrates. Our bodies need not only calories to provide us energy, but the right biochemical combination of nutrients to allow for proper metabolism. Micronutrient deficiency is when an individual has an insufficient intake of certain vitamins or minerals necessary for healthy functioning.

Target 2.1 also mentions infants, as nutrition during pregnancy can affect the gestating baby for life, highlighting the importance of breastfeeding for newborns.

Food insecurity, the focus of Indicator 2.1.2, is the ability of households and individuals to access food. Indicator 2.1.2 measures the percentage of individuals in the population who've experienced food insecurity, as measured by the Food Insecurity Experience Scale, a survey of eight questions.

A third of the global population experienced moderate or severe food insecurity as of 2021. Due to geographical isolation, acute hunger affects the most vulnerable regions of the world, characterised by the UN's lists of:

- least developed countries
- landlocked developing countries
- small island developing states

Development aid is a clear remedy to hunger, in the form of dietary supplements and foods fortified with micronutrients. Aid can help the development of sanitation systems to ensure drinking water and sewage don't mix, which can lead to infectious diseases causing undernourishment, compounded by dehydration from diarrheal diseases like dysentery. Developing countries also need healthcare coverage for those requiring intensive care for undernourishment.

Target 2.2

By 2030, end all forms of malnutrition, including achieving, by 2025, the internationally agreed Targets on stunting and wasting in children under 5 years of age, and address the nutritional needs of adolescent girls, pregnant and lactating women and older persons.

- Indicator 2.2.1: Prevalence of stunting (height for age <-2 standard deviation from the median of the World Health Organization (WHO) Child Growth Standards) among children under 5 years of age.
- Indicator 2.2.2: Prevalence of malnutrition (weight for height >+2 or <-2 standard deviation from the median of the WHO Child Growth Standards) among children under 5 years of age, by type (wasting and overweight).
- Indicator 2.2.3: Prevalence of anaemia in women aged 15 to 49 years, by pregnancy status (percentage).

Target 2.2 of the SDGs refers to a series of six maternal, infant and young child nutrition targets adopted by the World Health Organization in 2012 - among them a call for a 40% reduction of stunted children under 5 by 2025, and a 5% reduction of wasting by 2025.

The unit of measurement for Indicator 2.2.1 is for each year of age below 5, a ratio of height-to-weight, assessing if stunting has occurred, with a global aim to end stunting. Indicator 2.2.1 defines stunting by two standard deviations from the median of the WHO Child Growth Standards for height.

Indicator 2.2.2 measures two standard deviations from weight: underweight, in the form of wasting; and overweight, as childhood obesity - again aiming for zero prevalence by 2030.

Target 2.2 addresses the nutritional necessities of adolescent girls, and pregnant and lactating women, who may not absorb all vitamins and minerals from food. Indicator 2.2.3 focuses on anaemia, a treatable condition, by which lab testing reveals an individual's blood to be below a certain value of haemoglobin. This disallows the normal functioning of blood, the brain, and muscles, hindering one's ability for productive work, to earn income, and academic performance for children, with flow-on effects into adulthood. Severe anaemia carries with it a greater risk of death for the mother and child either before or after the birth. The measure is the proportion of women aged 15-49 years old with a concentration of haemoglobin below 110 grams per litre for pregnant women, and 120 grams per litre for lactating women. Women of reproductive age experience anaemia at disproportionate levels from menstruation, so ought to be targets for treatment for the benefit of furthering gender equality.

As of 2022, 22% of all children under 5 suffer from stunting (low height-for-age), down only 3% since 2015. This needs to come down another 8% to meet Target 2.2's 2025 aims.[12]

7% of children under five suffered from wasting, and a similar amount were overweight as of 2022. This will have to lower another 2% to meet Target 2.2 once 2025 data becomes available.[13]

Target 2.3

By 2030, double the agricultural productivity and incomes of small-scale food producers, in particular women, indigenous peoples, family farmers, pastoralists and fishers, including through secure and equal access to land, other productive resources and inputs, knowledge, financial services, markets and opportunities for value addition and non-farm employment.

- Indicator 2.3.1: The volume of production per labour unit by classes of farming/pastoral/forestry enterprise size.
- Indicator 2.3.2: Average income of small-scale food producers, by sex and indigenous status.

The cultivation of crops, and rearing of livestock, was not always inherent to human culture. It sprung forth when humans shifted from hunter-gatherer lifestyles to settling into fixed civilisations, tilling the land to make it arable to sow seeds. Humans domesticated animals around them on farms, and produced crop harvests to a surplus level, although in the modern era, agriculture has shifted from smallholdings to industrialised farms.

Target 2.3 is asking us to double agricultural productivity and crop yield of the bottom 40% of smallholders by land size, livestock, and revenue. At the time of writing, insufficient data was available to observe if a doubling of productivity or incomes of smallholders is on track at a regional or global level. The value of global agricultural output per worker in 2019 was $4,035 - an increase from the baseline in 2015 of $3,479.[14]

Target 2.4

By 2030, ensure sustainable food production systems and implement resilient agricultural practices that increase productivity and production, that help maintain ecosystems, that strengthen capacity for adaptation to climate change, extreme weather, drought, flooding and other disasters and that progressively improve land and soil quality.

- Indicator 2.4.1: Proportion of agricultural area under productive and sustainable agriculture.

Sustainable agriculture is a complex issue, and very much sensitive to the varied, unique agroecosystems, using advanced techniques to meet the challenges of:

- scarce freshwater resources
- erosion
- surface runoff
- salinisation
- imbalances in the environmental cycles of nitrogen, phosphate, and carbon
- slash-and-burn practices clearing forests

Organic farming is a form of sustainable agriculture, using natural manures, in contrast to synthetic fertilisers. Regenerative agriculture is another field receiving recent attention, an approach focusing on conservation of ecosystems. Standards and certifications have made recognising food grown in a sustainable way easier, for example organic certifications, the Rainforest Alliance and Fairtrade.

Without agriculture, our civilization never could have reached its current levels of population size. Advances in agronomy have proffered more food, fuel, and fibre for humankind. Agrochemicals, such as pesticides, keep pests away from crops, and synthetic fertilisers provide plants the chemical nutrients they need to grow.

But agricultural practices don't come without an environmental impact. Humans can neglect or ignore the welfare of animals. Agriculture continues to be a major driver of climate change - in its current form, the largest emitter of greenhouse gases after fossil fuels. Forests are crucial in heading off climate change, but deforestation still occurs on a massive scale to create pastures for grazing.

Can our aquifers, which sustain our vital freshwater supplies, contend with what agriculture draws from it, and pollutes into it? Will the degradation imposed on the Earth's land put us at greater risk of desertification, by which healthy soil mixtures, which used to support life, turn into drylands?

Can the environment handle what we take from it, and feed into it, or are we risking the depletion of resources necessary for human survival? Are we risking the compromise of the quality of our air, water, and soil - even entire ecosystems? Do our polluting patterns put at peril the destruction of habitats, and the extinction of species? Is the production of animal feed for livestock an inefficient use of precious resources? Have we placed ourselves higher on the food chain than necessary to live healthy lives? Do we need to slaughter cattle, pigs, and sheep? Antibiotics, growth hormones, and genetic engineering in the meat and dairy industry are affecting humans and animals alike.

We humans need fuel to work, raw materials to turn goods into necessary products, and grains, vegetables, and oils for cooking - but our policies and practices around agriculture need to change to be sustainable.

Only two countries - Belarus and Qatar - have so far reported on this Target's sole indicator. Belarus had 62% of agricultural land used in a productive and sustainable way, whereas Qatar had none.[15]

For further information regarding the transition to sustainable agriculture systems, I recommend the ongoing work of the FABLE Consortium, focused on food, agriculture, biodiversity, land-use and energy (FABLE).

Target 2.5

By 2020, maintain the genetic diversity of seeds, cultivated plants and farmed and domesticated animals and their related wild species, including through soundly managed and diversified seed and plant banks at the national, regional and international levels, and promote access to and fair and equitable sharing of benefits arising from the utilization of genetic resources and associated traditional knowledge, as internationally agreed.

- Indicator 2.5.1: Number of (a) plant and (b) animal genetic resources for food and agriculture secured in either medium- or long-term conservation facilities.
- Indicator 2.5.2: Proportion of local breeds classified as being at risk of extinction.

Gene banks can conserve genetic resources for food and agriculture, because biodiversity is necessary for food security. Seed banks are a type of gene bank for plants, to protect genetic biodiversity in agriculture. For animals, gene banks freeze sperm and egg cells of species. Gene banks keep such samples outside their natural environment (*ex situ*) rather than protected or managed on the farm (*in situ*).

As of 2022, 5.94 million unique plant genetic samples were in conservation facilities.[16] There was an increase between the start of the SDG period and 2020 of around half a million samples, suggesting Target 2.5's aim to maintain genetic diversity by 2020 was met by this measure.

Target 2.A

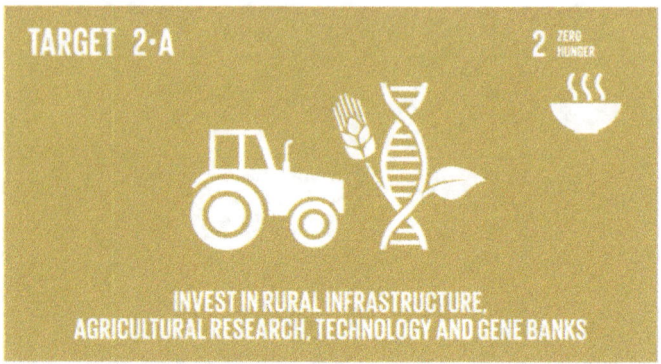

Increase investment, including through enhanced international cooperation, in rural infrastructure, agricultural research and extension services, technology development and plant and livestock gene banks in order to enhance agricultural productive capacity in developing countries, in particular least developed countries

- Indicator 2.a.1: The agriculture orientation index for government expenditures.
- Indicator 2.a.2: Total official flows (official development assistance plus other official flows) to the agriculture sector.

Investment is central to the SDGs, pointing toward the intergenerational aspect of the concept of sustainable development. In the developed world, investment suggests corporate profits dispensed as dividends, but for small-scale farmers, investment can be a hand on the bottom rung of the development ladder out of penury.

Government investment in agriculture needn't be financial, and can be physical capital, such as rural infrastructure. A small-scale farmer in the developing world must connect to markets to take part in the economy. If isolated from towns and cities, they need roads and railways. To see if the trip to the market will be worth the effort, depending on prices, access to telecommunications networks and electricity grids can save the farmer from travelling.

Governments can invest in human capital via education, imparting innovative farming techniques, skills, and the fruit of science and knowledge to improve yields by R&D.

Shocks from exchange rates from distant lands, fickle to the impact upon the developing world, can ruin lives and livelihoods. It's important for governments to act as public investors for their own agriculture, otherwise, what profit can a private investor expect to make upon a sector which isn't productive? This would be too risky, for the smallholder would be too likely to default on any financing received. Low-income governments need an investment strategy for agricultural development, due to agriculture's centrality to rural development and poverty alleviation, to increase productivity and income growth

For the purposes of Indicator 2.a.1, government spending on agriculture (including the forestry, fishing, and hunting sectors) includes policies and programs for:

- soil improvement and mitigating soil degradation
- managing animal health
- research on livestock and animal husbandry
- research on marine and freshwater biology
- afforestation and forestry.

For Indicator 2.a.2, we return to the topic of official development assistance (ODA). Indicator 2.a.2 mentions 'other official flows' - in the jargon of the OECD, these are official transactions not meeting the criteria of ODA, either because they're not aimed at financing sustainable development, or aren't concessional.

The OECD's Creditor Reporting System compares where aid from OECD donor countries has gone (i.e. which country or NGO), and the purpose the ODA was intended to serve. Indicator 2.a.2 focuses on transfers from donors to aid the recipient country's agricultural sector. The biggest recipient of official flows to agriculture as of 2022 was Egypt ($2 billion), more than twice as much as the next highest.[17]

Target 2.B

Correct and prevent trade restrictions and distortions in world agricultural markets, including through the parallel elimination of all forms of agricultural export subsidies and all export measures with equivalent effect, in accordance with the mandate of the Doha Development Round.

- Indicator 2.b.1: agricultural export subsidies.

The Doha Development Round are negotiations within the World Trade Organization (WTO), beginning in 2001 in Doha, Qatar, focused on lowering barriers to international trade. The WTO exists with the collective purpose of members lowering tariffs and trade barriers for goods and services, and sets out the procedures for settling disputes. Though not part of the UN System, 164 of the UN Member States are WTO Members.

Some of the contentions which hinder agreement between developed and developing countries in the context of trade centres on the topic of agriculture subsidies. Countries can adopt protectionist economic policies, such as taxes on imports or exports, and quotas, which other countries may consider put themselves at a relative disadvantage. In a free trade environment, other countries are going to want to know why any domestic support of income or prices by a trading partner was necessary.

An important WTO treaty in the context of Target 2.b is the Agreement on Agriculture, introducing us to another round of international trade negotiations: the Uruguay Round. The Uruguay Round was under the aegis of the General Agreement on Tariffs & Trade, the forebear of the WTO. The culmination of the Uruguay Round was the 1994 Marrakesh Agreement in Morocco, which established the WTO, and adopted the Agreement on Agriculture.

Subsidies are any benefits conferred by the government by transferring funds, or guaranteeing loans, and can include providing, or buying, goods or services (excluding infrastructure). Per the WTO Subsidies Agreement, members aren't to subsidise in a way which causes adverse effects to other members, which it calls an "injury to the domestic industry of another member." Article 6 of the Subsidies Agreement defines this as either subsidisation greater than 5% of its value, or debt forgiveness, including losses of an industry or business, except for once-off instances.

The world has managed to reach the aim of ending agricultural export subsidies as of 2021, down from $US217 million in 2015, achieving Target 2.b.[18]

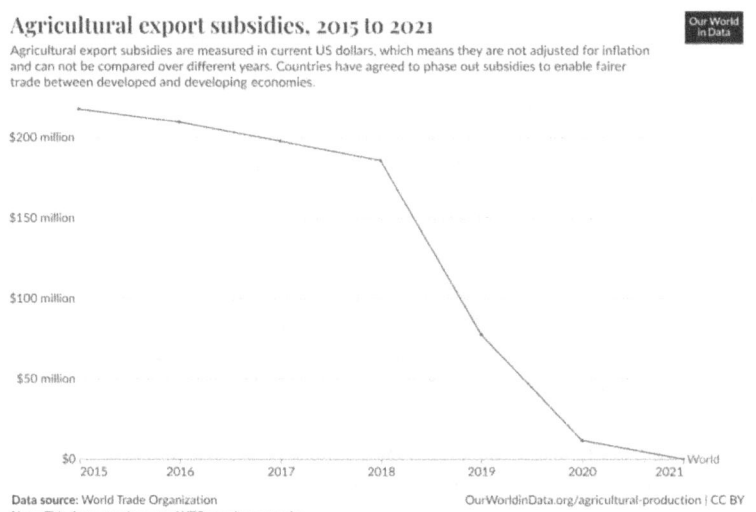

Target 2.C

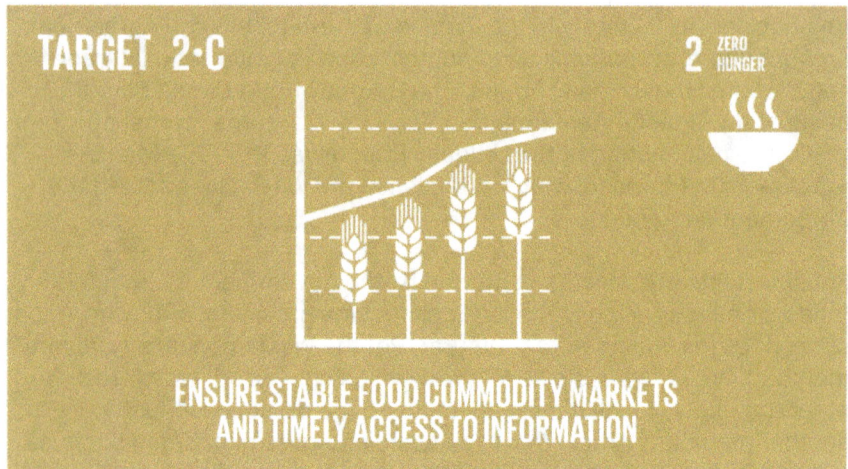

Adopt measures to ensure the proper functioning of food commodity markets and their derivatives and facilitate timely access to market information, including on food reserves, in order to help limit extreme food price volatility.

- Indicator 2.c.1: Indicator of food price anomalies.

An indicator of food price anomalies is a measure of market prices which deviate higher than normal, measured via a consumer price index (CPI), which tracks the inflation experienced by households, such as food expenditure.

The FAO uses the Food Price Monitoring and Analysis (FPMA), a tool which holds information and analyses of the consumer prices of basic foodstuffs over the years.

As of 2022, the country with by far the highest food price anomalies was Timor-Leste, with a score of 14.[19] To put this in context, the next highest was Hungary, which scored 4, with 0 suggesting normal prices.

Food reserves stored in a country can offset some of these price spikes, acting as a form of social protection to ensure resilient food systems.

Goal #3

To ensure healthy lives and promote well-being for all at all ages.

Target 3.1

By 2030, reduce the global maternal mortality ratio to less than 70 per 100,000 live births.

- Indicator 3.1.1: Maternal mortality ratio
- Indicator 3.1.2: Proportion of births attended by skilled health personnel

The definition of maternal death is a fatality occurring whilst a mother is pregnant, or within 42 days following the termination. The causes of maternal death can be manifold, including:

- post-partum bleeding, treated with intravenous blood transfusion in countries and communities with healthcare
- high blood pressure in the arteries because of the pregnancy
- proteinuria, an elevated level of proteins in the urine
- preeclampsia, a form of high blood pressure accompanied by proteinuria, related to pregnancy
- strokes, by which blood flow is unable to reach the brain in sufficient amounts, leading to cell death
- embolisms can form in the pulmonary artery, impeding the heart from sending blood toward the lungs
- amniotic fluid, which envelops the fetus in a sac during gestation, can enter the mother's bloodstream
- obstructed labour
- unsafe abortions
- HIV/AIDS, the leading cause of death during pregnancy and postpartum in countries with high prevalence

Many lives can be saved from the above complications, as most are preventable where healthcare solutions are available. Healthcare coverage tends to ensure an aseptic medical environment, free of pathogens, which can otherwise cause septic infections. Countries with low GDP per capita are more likely to have less healthcare coverage, making poverty an obvious risk factor for maternal mortality.

Fertility rates reflect a phenomenon by which the birth rates of poor countries are higher because of the poverty trap, emphasising the importance of meeting demand for access to modern forms of contraception.

The presence of skilled birth attendants can mitigate complications in the term of a pregnancy and childbirth, and prenatal care can function as a form of preventive healthcare.

Complementing the existence of health care coverage are public health campaigns, which can promote preventive behaviours, and mitigate the risks of maternal death.

The Millennium Development Goals, the UN goals which preceded the SDGs, had an entire goal devoted to maternal health: MDG #5. Target #5A of the MDGs was to "Reduce by three-quarters, between 1990 and 2015, the maternal mortality ratio."

The most recent global data for maternal mortality ratio at the time of writing is from 2020. There were 223 maternal deaths per 100,000 live births, down a little from the 2015 baseline of 219 per 100,000, and 342 per 100,000 at the start of the MDG period in 2000.[20] To reach Target 3.1's aim, we need to reduce this down to below 70 maternal deaths per 100,000 live births by 2030.

The proportion of births attended by skilled health attendants worldwide was 83% as of 2019, up from 62% in 2000.[21]

Target 3.2

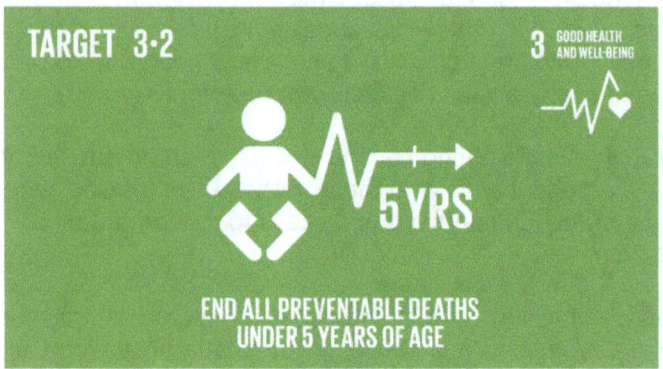

By 2030, end preventable deaths of newborns and children under 5 years of age, with all countries aiming to reduce neonatal mortality to at least as low as 12 per 1,000 live births and under-5 mortality to at least as low as 25 per 1,000 live births

- Indicator 3.2.1: Under-5 mortality rate
- Indicator 3.2.2: Neonatal mortality rate

The under-5 mortality rate measures the number of child deaths occurring within a population for every 1,000 live births under the age of 5. The leading causes of preventable deaths of children under 5 are infectious diseases, such as pneumonia, diarrhoea and malaria, as well as preterm births and complications during childbirth.[22]

The neonatal mortality rate measures the number of infant deaths in a population, excluding fetuses which did not survive the perinatal period during pregnancy and up to a year after birth. The definition of neonates, or newborns, for the purposes of Indicator 3.2.2, is within the first 28 days of birth - after which, the death of a child older than 28 days, but less than 5-years-old, would fit into the definition of Indicator 3.2.1.

As of 2022, the worldwide child mortality rate was 37 deaths per 1,000 live births, down from 42.6 in 2015 - still short of the 2030 aim of less than 25 deaths of children under-5 per 1,000 live births. For the neonatal mortality rate, with an aim of 12 neonatal deaths per 1,000 live births by 2030, the 2022 neonatal mortality rate is 17, down from 19.3 in 2015.[23]

Child mortality rate, 2022

The estimated share of newborns who die before reaching the age of five.

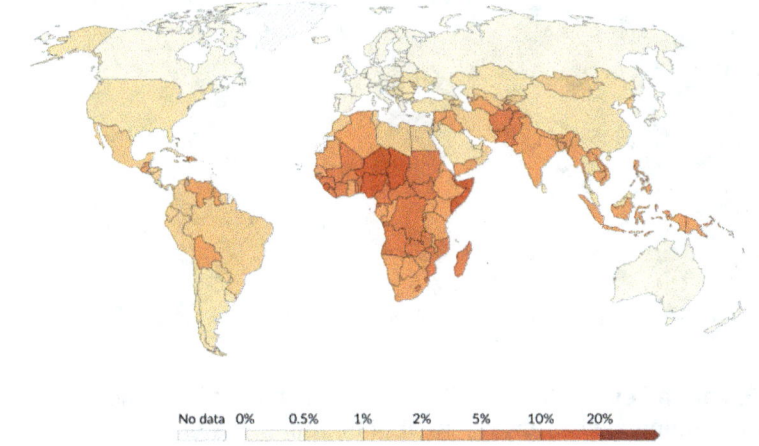

Data source: United Nations Inter-agency Group for Child Mortality Estimation (2024) OurWorldinData.org/child-mortality | CC BY

Neonatal mortality rate, 2022

The estimated share of newborns who die before reaching 28 days of age.

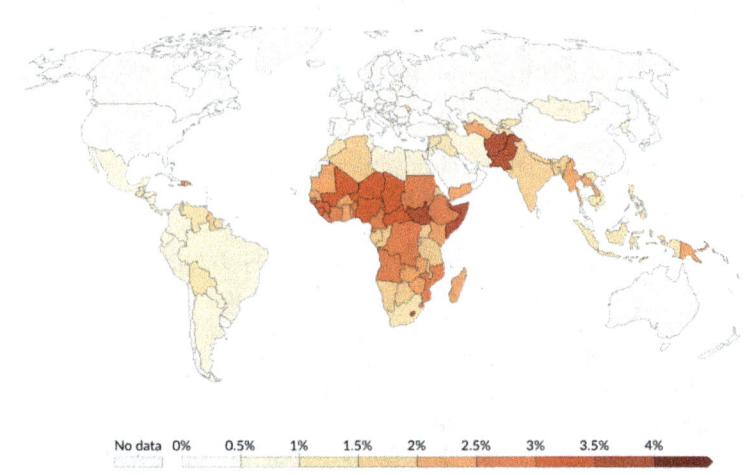

Data source: United Nations Inter-agency Group for Child Mortality Estimation (2024) OurWorldinData.org/child-mortality | CC BY

Target 3.3

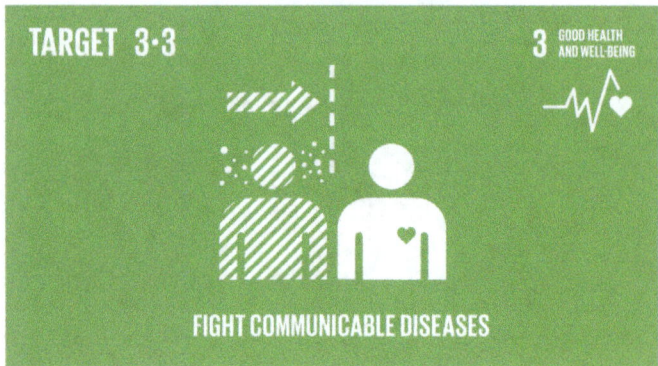

By 2030, end the epidemics of AIDS, tuberculosis, malaria and neglected tropical diseases and combat hepatitis, water-borne diseases and other communicable diseases.

- Indicator 3.3.1: Number of new HIV infections per 1,000 uninfected population
- Indicator 3.3.2: Tuberculosis per 100,000 population
- Indicator 3.3.3: Malaria incidence per 1,000 population
- Indicator 3.3.4: Hepatitis B incidence per 100,000 population
- Indicator 3.3.5: Number of people requiring interventions against neglected tropical disease

HIV/AIDS is a type of retrovirus, characterised by its ability to survive for long incubation periods, copying its RNA into a host's DNA.

The UN agency overseeing efforts to combat the HIV/AIDS pandemic is the Joint UN Programme on HIV/AIDS (UNAIDS), a joint effort of several UN agencies. As of 2023, 1.3 million people contract AIDS per year, resulting in 630,000 deaths, with 40 million people living with the virus.[24] A High-Level Meeting on AIDS declared the UN's intent to end AIDS by 2030, in alignment with SDG Target #3.3. But another major pandemic, COVID-19, has slowed progress. The 2023 global rate of new HIV infections of 0.17 per 1,000 uninfected people is short of the 2030 goal for elimination of HIV.[25]

A bacteria called *Mycobacterium tuberculosis* causes tuberculosis infections, transmitted via respiration, causing 10.8 million people a year to fall ill in 2023, killing 1.25 million.[26]

The World Health Organisation's Global Tuberculosis Programme works toward ridding the world of TB. The incidence of TB cases as of 2022 was 132 per population of 100,000, down from 142 per 100,000 in 2015.[27] Millennium Development Goal #6 was to "Combat HIV/AIDS, malaria and other diseases," and aimed to halve the incidence of AIDS, malaria, and TB by 2015, and reverse its incidence.

The world benefits from efforts such as the End TB Transmission Initiative, as part of the Stop TB Partnership, administered by the UN. Other impressive organisations in the fight against TB and AIDS - which are often co-morbidities alongside one another - are:

- The Global Fund to Fight AIDS, Tuberculosis and Malaria
- Unitaid
- IFFIm, in partnership with Gavi, the Vaccine Alliance.

One of the main strategies the World Health Organisation endorses for combating TB is DOTS (directly-observed treatment, short course), when a healthcare worker watches the patient take their dose. Immunisation with a TB vaccine is another widespread method of prevention, but strains of TB resistant to drugs used to treat the disease are hampering global efforts.

Alongside AIDS and TB, in 2023 there were 263 million cases of malaria, resulting in 597,000 deaths.[28] The mosquito-borne disease affects Sub-Saharan Africa to a disproportionate level, where it's home to most cases and deaths. In the effort to end the malaria pandemic, the world is still shy of the mark, with an incidence of 60 new cases per 1,000 people as of 2020.[29]

Indicator 3.3.4 focuses upon hepatitis B, a viral type of hepatitis, a disease characterised by inflammation of the liver, caused by an infection of the hepatitis B virus. Immunisations are an effective tool deployed worldwide to prevent its spread. The world isn't too far away from eliminating this disease, with less than 1% of children under-5 worldwide having tested positive for an active case of hepatitis B as of 2020.[30]

Indicator 3.3.5 looks at neglected tropical diseases. These infections are common to developing countries in the tropics and subtropics of Africa, Asia, and the Americas, and include:

- parasitic worms - microscopic in size, causing lymphatic filariasis, which affects the lymphatic system
- schistosomiasis - caused by parasitic worms
- soil-transmitted helminthiasis - caused by another parasitic worm, in this case observable to the human eye. These types of worms, called helminths, infect the intestines, and are transmissible via the soil in which they live.
- onchocerciasis - a disease of the eyes and skin, also caused by a worm
- African sleeping sickness - also known as human African Trypanosomiasis
- leishmaniasis - a parasite spread by sandflies
- mycetoma - a bacterial and fungal infection, spread by the skin's exposure to soil or water containing the bacteria or fungus causing this disease.
- yaws - a chronic skin infection, resulting in small lumps and ulcers on the skin
- dracunculiasis - caused by the worm-like parasite *Dracunculus*, also known as Guinea worm, named after the Gulf of Guinea in West Africa, where it was once prevalent
- echinococcosis - caused by parasitic worms.

Included among the neglected tropical diseases is snake envenoming, caused by the toxins from a snakebite.

One of the strategies endorsed by the World Health Organisation for the neglected tropical diseases caused by helminth worms is preventive, whereby health workers administer chemotherapy medications to populations susceptible to infection by these worms.

Neglected tropical diseases are down 150 million since 2015, to a 2021 total of 1.65 billion as of 2021.[31]

Water-borne diseases, mentioned in the Target, though not measured by an Indicator, are often diarrheal, including dysentery, typhoid, giardiasis or infections from *E. coli* and Salmonella.

Target 3.4

By 2030, reduce by one third premature mortality from non-communicable diseases through prevention and treatment and promote mental health and well-being

- Indicator 3.4.1: Mortality rate attributed to cardiovascular disease, cancer, diabetes or chronic respiratory disease
- Indicator 3.4.2: Suicide mortality rate

Non-communicable diseases are those for which a pathogen infecting the host isn't responsible. As Indicator 3.4.1 makes clear, the most well-known non-communicable diseases are those affecting the heart and blood vessels, diabetes, cancer, and respiratory diseases such as chronic obstructive lung disease.

How do we measure well-being, or quality of life, and the mental aspects? An empirical score exists in the form of the World Happiness Report, though Indicator 3.4.2 uses the total opposite of wellbeing, suicide. The global suicide rate in 2019 was 9.1 deaths per 100,000 people, down only a fraction since 2015.[32]

As of 2019, the expected share of deaths worldwide from non-communicable diseases was 18%, down 1% from 2015 - far from the aim to reduce premature mortality from non-communicable diseases by one-third.[33]

Target 3.5

Strengthen the prevention and treatment of substance abuse, including narcotic drug abuse and harmful use of alcohol.

- Indicator 3.5.1: Coverage of treatment interventions (pharmacological, psychosocial and rehabilitation and aftercare services) for substance use disorders.
- Indicator 3.5.2: Alcohol per capita consumption (aged 15 years and older) within a calendar year in litres of pure alcohol

The UN agencies overseeing the topic of substance abuse are the World Health Organisation and UNODC (UN Office on Drugs and Crime), which oversees the three main International Drug Control Conventions.

To support UN Member States to treat drug and alcohol use disorders in an ethical, evidence-based way, the World Health Organisation and UNODC have formulated:

- International Standards for the Treatment of Drug Use Disorders
- International Guide for Monitoring Alcohol Consumption and Related Harm

The World Health Organisation collects data for all Member States' per capita alcohol consumption over age 15. As of 2019, the biggest consumers were Romania, Georgia, Czech Republic and Latvia, drinking more than 13 litres of pure alcohol per capita.[34] Only country-level data is available for alcohol use disorders, and to see if treatment interventions have been strengthened, per Target 3.5's aim, but as of 2019, global alcohol consumption per person has reduced a little since 2015.

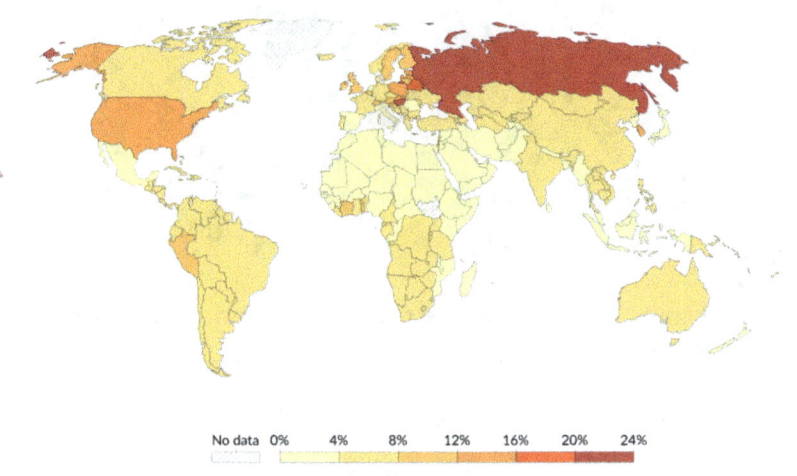

Share of population with alcohol use disorders, 2016
The percentage of people aged over 15 who have had an alcohol use disorder[1] within the last year.

Data source: World Health Organization
OurWorldinData.org/alcohol-consumption | CC BY

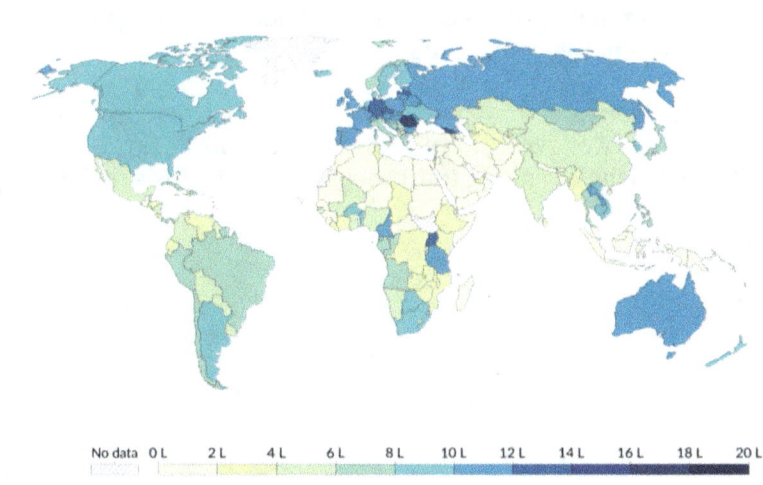

Alcohol consumption per person, 2019
Estimated consumption of alcohol is measured in liters of pure alcohol per person aged 15 or older, per year.

Data source: Multiple sources compiled by World Bank (2024)
OurWorldinData.org/alcohol-consumption | CC BY

Target 3.6

By 2020, halve the number of global deaths and injuries from road traffic accidents

- Indicator 3.6.1: Death rate due to road traffic injuries

The number of global deaths from traffic collisions was 1.35 million in 2016, which was reduced to 1.2 million in 2021, missing the 2020 aim of Target 3.6 for a halving of fatalities.[35]

Road traffic injuries are the main cause of death for people aged 15-29 worldwide, and are the eighth leading cause of death for all age groups, estimated to become seventh by 2030.

As of 2019, the death rate from road traffic injuries has reduced only 0.3 per 100,000 people worldwide, from 17 deaths per 100,000 in 2015, far off track from the aim of halving traffic deaths by 2020, missing Target 3.6.[36]

Target 3.7

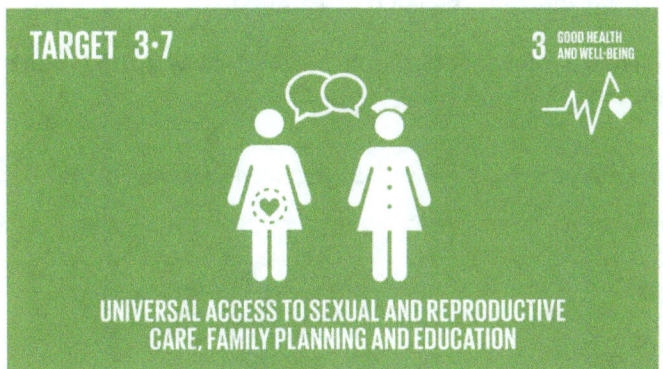

By 2030, ensure universal access to sexual and reproductive health-care services, including for family planning, information and education, and the integration of reproductive health into national strategies and programs

- Indicator 3.7.1: Percentage of married women ages 15–49 years whose need for family planning is satisfied with modern methods of contraception.
- Indicator 3.7.2: Adolescent birth rate (aged 10–14 years; aged 15–19 years) per 1,000 women in that age group.

The UN agency overseeing sexual and reproductive health is UNFPA, otherwise known as the UN Population Fund.

To help meet the rights to access affordable and quality sexual and reproductive health services, the World Health Organisation has published a family planning health care handbook, providing developing countries guidance on contraceptive methods.

Among the consequences for failing to acknowledge the unmet demand for contraceptive choices, more mouths will need greater levels of foreign aid, but reducing fertility rates in the least developed countries could slow down the rapid rise of populations. This phenomenon is known as the 'demographic transition,' of which meeting family planning and contraceptive needs is a key pillar in the least developed countries.

Indicator 3.7.2 focuses on adolescent birth rates. As of 2023, 77% of women worldwide were able to meet their family planning needs, still short of the universal access aim of Target 3.7.[37]

The worldwide adolescent birth rate, as of 2024, was 1.5 births per 1,000 10-14-year-olds.[38]

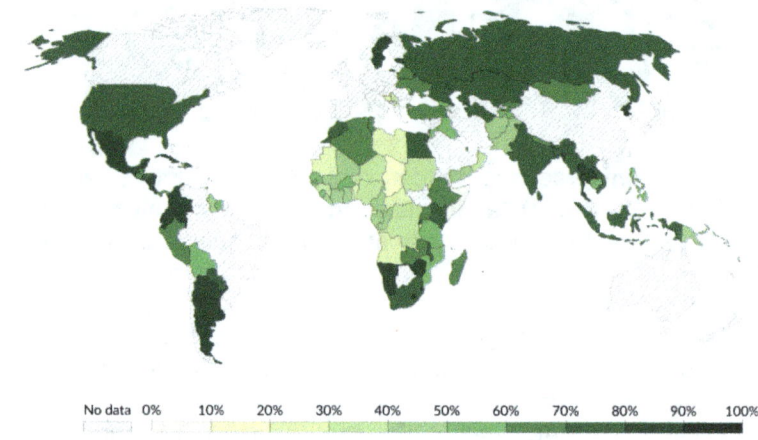

Share of women whose family planning needs are met, 2021

The proportion of women of reproductive age (15-49 years) who are currently using at least one modern contraceptive[1] method, out of the total population of women who have demand for family planning[2] methods.

Data source: Population Division, Department of Economic and Social Affairs and United Nations Population Fund
OurWorldinData.org/fertility-rate | CC BY

Target 3.8

Achieve universal health coverage, including financial risk protection, access to quality essential health-care services and access to safe, effective, quality and affordable essential medicines and vaccines for all

- Indicator 3.8.1: Coverage of essential health services.
- Indicator 3.8.2: Proportion of population with large household expenditures on health as a share of total household expenditure or income

The international community needs to finance healthcare services for the 692 million people living below $2.15 a day as of 2024.[39]

The measure of coverage for essential health services includes 14 World Health Organization indicators for:

- family planning
- pregnancy care
- child immunisation
- treatment of children
- tuberculosis
- HIV/AIDS
- malaria
- water, sanitation, and hygiene (WASH)
- hypertension
- diabetes
- tobacco

- hospital access
- health workforce
- health security

These indicators form an index of coverage of essential health services, on a scale of 0 to 100, the measure used for Indicator 3.8.1. As of 2021, the world result for the index of coverage of essential health services stands at 67 out of 100, still far from the 2030 goal of universal health coverage, the aim of SDG #3.[40]

Indicator 3.8.2 measures the proportion of household income spent on healthcare, using two thresholds of financial hardship. The lower one is for 10% of household income spent on healthcare, and the higher threshold for a quarter of household income spent on healthcare, which can place a household at financial risk in paying for any healthcare needs. As of 2019, 3% of the world population spent more than a quarter of household expenditure on health, and 13% for more than 10%.[41]

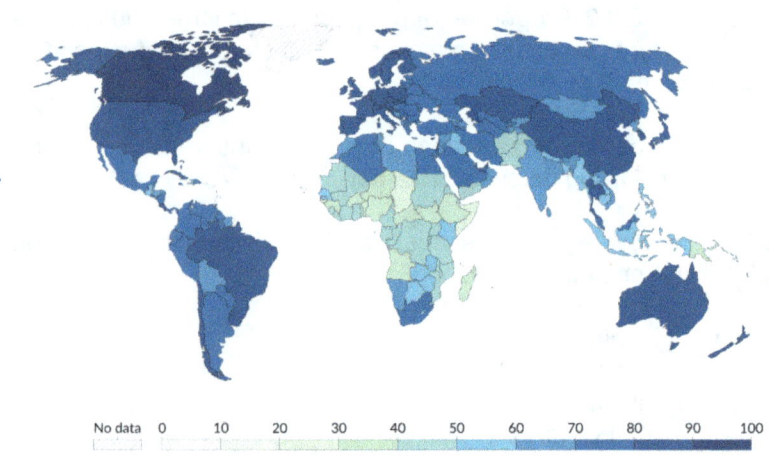

Target 3.9

By 2030, substantially reduce the number of deaths and illnesses from hazardous chemicals and air, water and soil pollution and contamination

- Indicator 3.9.1: Mortality rate attributed to the household (indoor) and ambient (outdoor) air pollution.
- Indicator 3.9.2: Mortality rate attributed to unsafe water, sanitation, and lack of hygiene.
- Indicator 3.9.3: Mortality rate attributed to unintentional poisoning.

Air pollution is a cause of death responsible for infections, cancers and chronic diseases of the respiratory system, heart disease, and stroke.

PM2.5 is particulate matter of a diameter of 2.5 micrometres or less, exposure of which - from both outdoors and household air pollution - poses great risks to health. 2.1 billion people worldwide cook using open fires or stoves burning dirty fuels, resulting in an estimated 3.2 million annual deaths.[42] The saddest aspect is such individuals wish to have access to energy, but the only form accessible to them compromises their air quality and health. The air in people's homes is killing millions, due to the burning of solid cooking fuels like wood, despite its use since the times of the earliest humans. Other fuels which put populations at risk in the home from burning are animal dung, charcoal, agricultural waste, and inefficient kerosene stoves.

As of 2019, the global death rate from household and ambient air pollution was 104 per 100,000 people, 18 deaths per 100,000 from unsafe water, sanitation and hygiene, and 1 death from unintentional poisoning per 100,000.[43] With only 2019 data available, we cannot tell if there's been a substantial reduction of deaths and illnesses from hazardous chemicals and pollution.

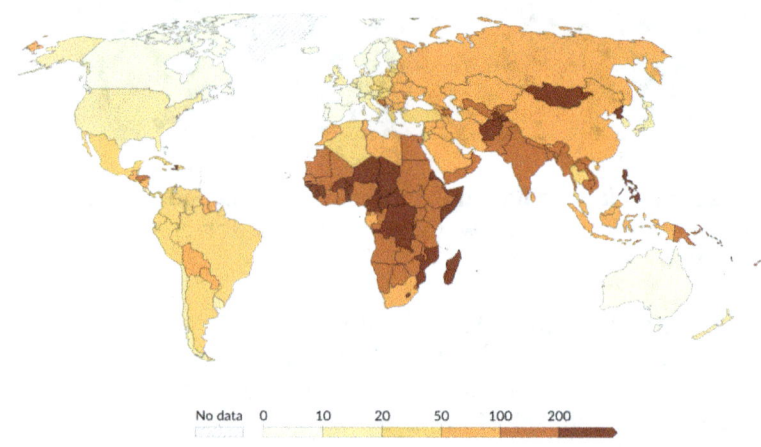

Target 3.A

Strengthen the implementation of the World Health Organization Framework Convention on Tobacco Control in all countries, as appropriate

- Indicator 3.a.1: Age-standardized prevalence of current tobacco use among persons aged 15 years and older

The FCTC, or WHO Framework Convention on Tobacco Control, is an international treaty, adopted in 2005 at the World Health Assembly, which is the decision-making body of the WHO.

In the West, we're most familiar with tobacco in the form of cigarettes. But around the world, diverse cultures have many ways to adapt the *Nicotiana* plant from the nightshade family, such as Indonesian kretek, blended with cloves. Snus is popular in Sweden and Norway - a form of dipping tobacco, placed between the lip and the gum. Smokeless forms of tobacco go by many names throughout India and South Asia. One of these is gutkha, a combination of tobacco, calcium hydroxide, a tree extract, nuts from the areca palm tree, and leaves of the betel tree. Though smokeless, these products still pose a medical threat and are carcinogenic.

Global share of tobacco use was 23% as of 2020, not much down since 2015, suggesting implementation efforts of the FCTC need to be further strengthened.[44]

Target 3.B

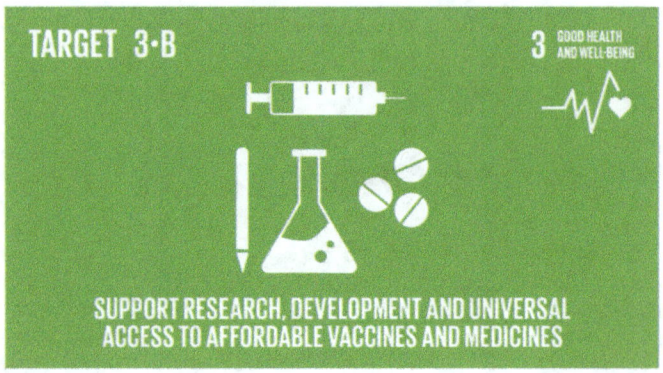

Support the research and development of vaccines and medicines for the communicable and non-communicable diseases that primarily affect developing countries, provide access to affordable essential medicines and vaccines, in accordance with the Doha Declaration on the TRIPS Agreement and Public Health, which affirms the right of developing countries to use to the full the provisions in the Agreement on Trade-Related Aspects of Intellectual Property Rights regarding flexibilities to protect public health, and, in particular, provide access to medicines for all.

- Indicator 3.b.1: Proportion of the target population covered by all vaccines included in their national program.
- Indicator 3.b.2: Total net official development assistance (ODA) to medical research and basic health sectors.
- Indicator 3.b.3: Proportion of health facilities that have a core set of relevant essential medicines available and affordable on a sustainable basis.

We explored the Doha Declaration earlier within Target 2.b. The focus of the Doha Declaration for Target 3.b is the World Trade Organization's TRIPS Agreement, which stands for Trade-Related Aspects of Intellectual Property Rights. The TRIPS Agreement is an annex of the 1994 Marrakesh Agreement, already discussed in Target 2.b. The TRIPS Agreement enforces intellectual property (IP) rights worldwide, relating to authors of creative works, and all manner of copyrights, patents, and trademarks. The nature of the Doha Declaration on the TRIPS Agreement and Public Health is to recognise public health in developing countries ought to take precedence over IP rights. IP is a very important aspect of drug discovery, but pharmaceutical companies need to balance profits with public health considerations when pricing medicines and vaccines in the developing countries. The least developed countries are the most afflicted by the epidemics of HIV/AIDS, TB and malaria, so have the most urgent need for access to affordable treatments.

Alongside the World Trade Organization, the UN agency whose work is relevant to Target 3.b is the World Intellectual Property Organization (WIPO).

The definitions of vaccine coverage in Indicator 3.b.1 are those recommended by the World Health Organization and UNICEF, including:

- two doses of measles
- a full schedule of human papilloma virus (HPV)
- pneumococcal disease
- diphtheria, three doses of pertussis, and tetanus (DPT)

As of 2021, 81% of one-year-olds worldwide have immunisations of the DPT vaccine, a 4% decrease since 2015.[45] 71% of children worldwide had vaccinations for measles as of 2021, up from 63% in 2015.[46] 51% of one-year-olds had vaccinations for pneumococcal disease in 2021, up from 38% in 2015.[47] Worldwide, 15% of adolescent girls had vaccinations for HPV as of 2022, up from 9% in 2015.

The OECD's Creditor Reporting System shows the amounts donors gave each year of their total ODA to which sector. In this instance, we want to see how many millions of dollars donor countries gave to the basic health sector and medical research of developing countries - in 2022, the least developed countries received $6.45 billion in ODA for these purposes.[48]

The World Health Organization selects essential medicines into the Model Lists, including Essential Medicines for Children. The intention is for enough essential medicines to be available at health facilities for affordable prices, which may otherwise be out of reach of the daily wages of some living below national poverty lines.

Target 3.C

Substantially increase health financing and the recruitment, development, training, and retention of the health workforce in developing countries, especially in the least developed countries and small island developing states.

- Indicator 3.c.1: Health worker density and distribution

Though Indicator 3.c.1 measures the number of nurses, midwives, dentists, pharmacists and medical doctors in a population, there's only data at the global level for the latter, and national data for the others. As of 2022, there were 1.7 medical doctors per 1,000 people in the world, 0.3 for the low-income countries, and 1.4 for middle-income countries.[49] As there aren't earlier data points in the SDG period, we're unable to tell if there's been an increase in the recruitment of medical doctors.

An initiative which aims to bridge this gap to universal health coverage is the One Million Community Health Workers Campaign, whose mission is to recruit, train and equip one million health workers to work in rural communities in Sub-Saharan Africa, in partnership with the UN and others.

Target 3.D

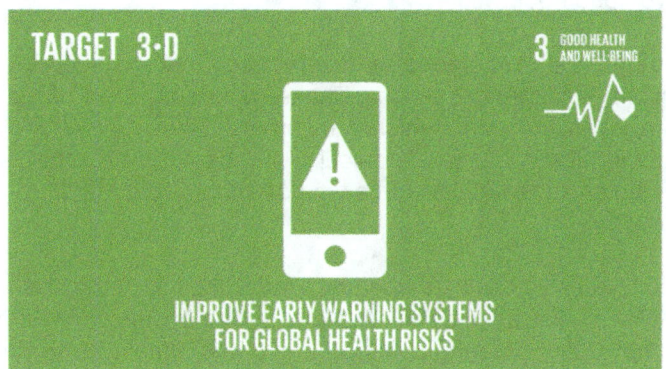

Strengthen the capacity of all countries, in particular developing countries, for early warning, risk reduction and management of national and global health risks.

- Indicator 3.d.1: International Health Regulations (IHR) capacity and health emergency preparedness
- Indicator 3.d.2: Percentage of bloodstream infections due to selected antimicrobial resistant organisms.

Target 3.d and its Indicators look at health security, inclusive of emergency management, aiming to increase the ability of all World Health Organisation member states to prepare for, or prevent, public health emergencies across international borders.

The World Health Organization's International Health Regulations (IHR) guides states-parties, obliging them to self-report each year on their adherence and capacities toward the IHR. The self-assessment tool has 15 indications, including:

- legislation
- financing
- zoonotic diseases of human-animal crossover, which account for 75% of emerging pathogens[50]
- coordination between countries to notify one another of events which may pose a global health risk
- food safety
- preventing and controlling infections

As can be seen in the below graph, as of 2023, global IHR capacities have weakened overall from the 2015 baseline, with similar trends in the least developed countries.[51]

Indicator 3.d.2 looks at bloodstream infections due to selected antimicrobial-resistant organisms. These include a variety of the bacterium *Staphylococcus,* which can sometimes be resistant to the antibiotic methicillin, a type of penicillin. The bacterium *E. coli* also produces an enzyme resistant to a type of antibiotics called cephalosporins.

Clinical laboratories can test whether a microorganism may be susceptible to resistance of an antibiotic, which occurs when viruses, bacteria, fungi, and parasites change, and drugs once used to treat them either have less efficacy, or no longer work. This makes it harder to treat infections of such microorganisms, allowing for the possibility of the diseases they cause to become more lethal.

For Indicator 3.d.2, the global share of *Staphylococcus aureus* infections resistant to methicillin stood at 31% as of 2021, up from 20% in 2016. *E. coli* infections resistant to cephalosporins stood at a global total of 39% in 2021, up from 35% in 2016, doubling in 2018, before coming back down.[52]

Goal #4

Ensure inclusive and equitable quality education and promote lifelong learning opportunities for all.

Target 4.1

By 2030, ensure that all girls and boys complete free, equitable and quality primary and secondary education leading to a relevant and effective learning outcome.

- Indicator 4.1.1: Proportion of children and young people (a) in grade 2/3; (b) at the end of primary; and (c) at the end of lower secondary achieving at least a minimum proficiency level in (i) reading and (ii) Mathematics, by sex
- Indicator 4.1.2: Completion rate (primary education, lower secondary education, upper secondary education)

One of the overarching aims of SDG #2 is to end Learning Poverty, which the World Bank defines as 10-year-olds being unable to read and understand a simple story.

Indicator 4.1.1 looks at 'minimum proficiency levels,' the benchmark of basic knowledge, as measured by assessments - in this instance, for reading and mathematics. Indicator 4.1.1 looks at reading and maths skills at three points: grade 2 and 3; end of primary schooling; and end of lower secondary.

'Performance level descriptors' describe the knowledge and skills shown by students at each of the above levels, helping to assess students across countries. Below are a handful of examples of the respective descriptors for each grade:

- Reading, grade 3: Read written words aloud, understanding the meaning of sentences and short texts and naming the topic.
- Maths, grades 2/3: To make sense of, calculate numbers, and recognise shapes.
- Maths, end of primary: Basic measurement and reading and creating graphs.
- Maths, end of lower secondary school: Solving maths problems, using tables and graphs, as well as algebra.

The data for assessing trends in students draws from a half-dozen surveys, to test the effectiveness of learning outcomes, as in some countries, it's possible for a student to pass through grades without meeting the 'minimum proficiency levels.' The benefit of these surveys is they serve as tools to provide the evidence toward making decisions to improve education.

As of 2023, half of all students worldwide at the end of primary education met 'minimum proficiency levels' in reading and maths, the same as at the start of the SDG period in 2015. For lower secondary in 2019, 48% met the minimum proficiency level for reading, and 39% in mathematics, a couple percentage increase since 2015.

The second Indicator for this Target looks at school completion of primary, lower secondary and upper secondary. The completion rate for primary education worldwide was 88% as of 2022, up only 3% since 2015.[53] Lower secondary completion rates were 77% in 2023, again up only 2% since 2015.[54] Global upper secondary completion was 59% as of 2023, up 6% since 2015.[55] These results imply all children won't complete primary and secondary completion by 2030.

Target 4.2

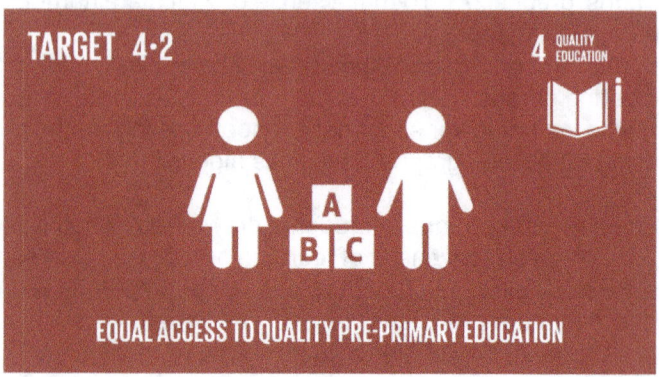

By 2030, ensure that all girls and boys have access to quality early childhood development, care, and pre-primary education so that they are ready for primary education

- Indicator 4.2.1: Proportion of children aged 24–59 months who are developmentally on track in health, learning and psychosocial well-being, by sex
- Indicator 4.2.2: Participation rate in organised learning (one year before the official primary entry age), by sex

The UN agency responsible for Indicator 4.2.1 is UNICEF (United Nations Children's Fund), focused upon children. UNICEF's Early Childhood Development Index 2030 is a tool to measure Indicator 4.2.1's progress, as the science underlying early childhood development has revealed it as a crucial intervention leading to outcomes through to adulthood.

Worldwide, as of 2023, only 66% of children aged 3 to 5 are on track in health, learning and psychosocial well-being.[56]

Indicator 4.2.2. looks at pre-school. As of 2022, global enrolment in organised learning was 72% of children at the age of one year before primary entry, the same as 2015, off-track for universal pre-primary education by 2030.[57] Disaggregated per the definition of the indicator, worldwide enrolment was at parity for boys and girls as of 2023.[58]

Target 4.3

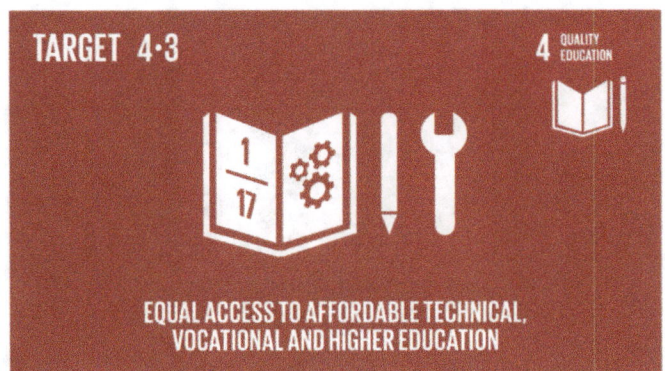

By 2030, ensure equal access for all women and men to affordable and quality technical, vocational and tertiary education, including university

- Indicator 4.3.1: Participation rate of youth and adults in formal and non-formal education and training in the previous 12 months, by sex

To coincide with the adoption of the Sustainable Development Goals in 2015, the UN released a report entitled Education 2030 alongside the Incheon Declaration and Framework for Action (named after the Korean city, Incheon), which reinforces the purposes of SDG #2. In its vision for education toward 2030, it highlights aspects of SDG #4 most relevant to Target 4.3, including inclusion and equity, gender equality and lifelong learning opportunities.

Tertiary education can be vocational, which imparts skills onto the prospective worker for direct application to employment; or university, which tends to focus more on theoretical knowledge.

The worldwide enrolment rate for tertiary education as of 2022 was 41%, up from 36% in 2015, though the data available isn't disaggregated by sex.[59]

Target 4.4

By 2030, substantially increase the number of youth and adults who have relevant skills, including technical and vocational skills, for employment, decent jobs and entrepreneurship

- Indicator 4.4.1: Proportion of youth and adults with information and communications technology (ICT) skills, by type of skill

The mention of ICT in Indicator 4.4.1 introduces us to the UN agency specialising in this field, the International Telecommunication Union (ITU).

The ICT skills measured for Indicator 4.4.1 range from as simple as copying and pasting, to writing computer programs in a programming language. It's imperative across countries for individuals and households to have access to, and use ICTs, to fulfil the ambitions of SDG #8 (Decent work and economic growth). The world must progress toward greater connection, reflective of the value of digital knowledge, and the information societies we've become. Telecommunication is key to development, the importance of ICTs extending beyond the individual and household, to education. ICTs also offer opportunities for governments and enterprises, and the infrastructure for this needs to be there to begin with.

There's only country level data to see if there's been a substantial increase in skills before 2030.

Target 4.5

By 2030, eliminate gender disparities in education and ensure equal access to all levels of education and vocational training for the vulnerable, including persons with disabilities, indigenous peoples and children in vulnerable situations

- Indicator 4.5.1: Parity indices (female/male, rural/urban, bottom/top wealth quintile and others such as disability status, indigenous peoples and conflict-affected, as data become available) for all education Indicators on this list that can be disaggregated

For Indicator 4.5.1, there's not one global parity index for gender equality, disability, and Indigenous people, but there is data for individual countries.

Those with a gender parity for primary completion lower than 0.8 (i.e. less than 8 girls for every 10 boys) were, Central African Republic, Yemen and Somalia, and Niger and Afghanistan had parities closer to 7 girls for every boy.[60]

For secondary completion, a half-dozen other countries in sub-Saharan Africa with 2024 data had either gender parity, or rates favouring girls.[61] The lowest secondary completion gender parities were in Chad and Afghanistan, where half as many girls completed secondary per boy.

Target 4.6

By 2030, ensure that all youth and a substantial proportion of adults, both men and women, achieve literacy and numeracy

- Indicator 4.6.1: Proportion of population in a given age group achieving at least a fixed level of proficiency in functional (a) literacy and (b) numeracy skills, by sex

Indicator 4.6.1 introduces the concept of 'fixed level of proficiency,' a standard of knowledge in a field of learning - in this instance, measuring literacy and numeracy.

To survey the skills of adults, the OECD runs the PIAAC (Programme for the International Assessment of Adult Competencies), assessing adults in literacy and numeracy.

The worldwide literacy rates of people between 15-24 years old as of 2022 - disaggregated by sex, as defined by the indicator - were 94% for men and 92% for women, an increase since 2015 of a couple percent.[62]

The worldwide literacy rate for males over 15 was 90% in 2022, and 83% for females, but there's insufficient recent data across countries to form a global numeracy rate to observe progress toward 2030.[63]

Target 4.7

By 2030, ensure that all learners acquire the knowledge and skills needed to promote sustainable development, including, among others, through education for sustainable development and sustainable lifestyles, human rights, gender equality, promotion of a culture of peace and non-violence, global citizenship and appreciation of cultural diversity and of culture's contribution to sustainable development

- Indicator 4.7.1: Extent to which (i) global citizenship education and (ii) education for sustainable development are mainstreamed in (a) national education policies; (b) curricula; (c) teacher education; and (d) student assessment

For us to have peace and sustainable development, we first need to educate ourselves on what sustainable development is. The issues the SDGs place before us are urgent, but we can foster sustainable development, to keep at bay the most sudden and striking outcomes on our planet. Our world is interdependent, and whether we choose to be or not, we are global citizens.

But what is a good global citizen? Like anything in life, to light the way, we need an education in global citizenship. We can then go on to contribute, whatever our age, and this opportunity ought to inspire us all. Education to foster understanding across countries, as well as being a human right, opens a world of freedom for the learner.

The responsibility to put in place this right of citizens in each country lies with the relevant ministries of education, but we have an opportunity at the international level for member states to cooperate via UNESCO's efforts.

UNESCO has issued a recommendation document, outlining how governments should foster education for sustainable development and global citizenship. Recommendations are part of the legal jargon of UNESCO to set standards for member states to put into practice or law.

The results for Indicator 4.7.1 are encouraging among the countries with data, measuring the extent of mainstreaming global citizenship and sustainable development education. The unit of measure is an index, where 0 is the worst, and 1 the best. Most reporting countries record indexes greater than 0.8 for mainstreaming of global citizenship and sustainable development in national education, with comparable results for mainstreaming in curricula, teacher education and student assessment.[64]

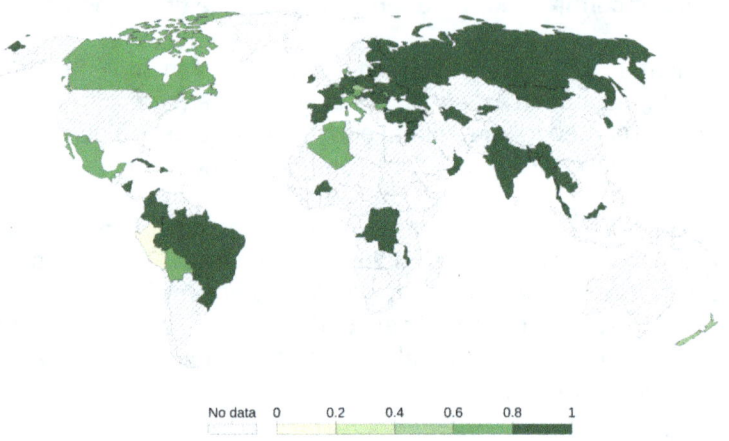

Target 4.A

Build and upgrade education facilities that are child, disability and gender sensitive and provide safe, non-violent, inclusive and effective learning environments for all

- Indicator 4.a.1: Proportion of schools offering basic services, by type of service

Information and communication technologies allow even the remotest schools and children to access the best education institutions in the world. But schools need electricity to power ICTs, and an internet connection and computers for teaching and learning - all solutions available at low-cost. The infrastructure of the learning environment needs to adapt to be suitable for those with a disability, factoring in learning materials for disabled students. School facilities need basic facilities too, for drinking water, sanitation, and handwashing.

The proportion of schools offering the basic service of access to electricity as of 2022 was 90% in upper secondary, and 77% in primary. 81% of secondary schools offered access to handwashing facilities, and 77% of primary schools.[65] 86% of secondary schools offered access to drinking water, and 77% of primary schools.[66] 80% of upper secondary schools offered access to computers, and 49% of primary schools. The proportion of primary schools offering internet access for the purposes of teaching worldwide in 2022 was 44%.[67] 91% of secondary schools offered single-sex toilets worldwide in 2022, and 79% of primary schools.[68]

Target 4.B

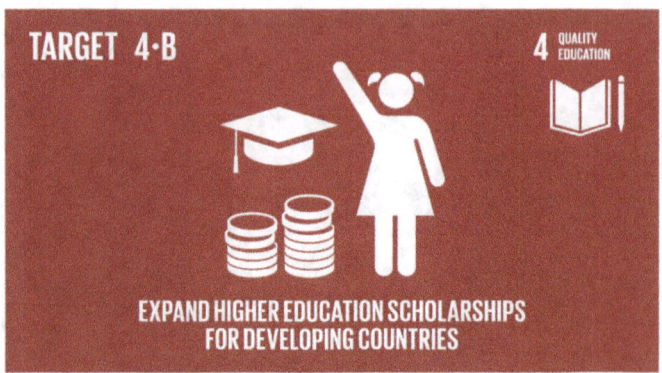

By 2020, substantially expand globally the number of scholarships available to developing countries, in particular least developed countries, small island developing States and African countries, for enrolment in higher education, including vocational training and information and communications technology, technical, engineering and scientific programmes, in developed countries and other developing countries

- Indicator 4.b.1: Volume of official development assistance flows for scholarships by sector and type of study

Indicator 4.b.1 reintroduces the concept of official development assistance (ODA), in this instance, ODA earmarked for scholarships to finance the development of education systems.

Indicator 4.b.1 looks at development flows to the respective regions mentioned in the body of Target 4.b. For African countries, as of 2022, ODA intended for scholarships was $US305 million, an increase from $US225 million from 2015.[69] For the least developed countries, 2022 scholarship aid was $235 million, down by $10 million since 2015. For the Small Island Developing States, scholarship aid was $53 million in 2022, down from $104 million in 2015.

2020 has passed, and there was only an increase between 2015 and 2020 in Africa among the above regions - without defining how to measure a substantial expansion - with no worldwide data available.

Target 4.C

By 2030, substantially increase the supply of qualified teachers, including through international cooperation for teacher training in developing countries, especially least developed countries and small island developing States

- Indicator 4.c.1: Proportion of teachers with the minimum required qualifications, by education level

Teachers in developing countries are among the most valuable resources in a country's education system, and the lever upon which economic development begins. As such, it's important teachers are effective, to ensure students' learning outcomes are too. As of 2019, the proportion of pre-primary teachers with 'minimum required qualifications' was 65% in the least developed countries (LDCs), 73% in the small island developing countries (SIDS), and 85% worldwide in 2022.[70] Neither of these measures showed a substantial increase in the SDG period.

For primary school teachers, the 2022 proportion was 89% for SIDS, and 73% for LDCs in 2021.[71] The worldwide proportion was 85%, the same since 2015, off track for a substantial increase before 2030. For lower secondary schools, 84% of teachers had the 'minimum required qualifications' worldwide in 2021, and 64% for LDCs, and 88% for SIDS in 2020.[72] For upper secondary, 86% of teachers in the SIDS were qualified in 2020, 86% worldwide in 2021, and 62% in LDCs in 2019.[73] There's no earlier worldwide figure for secondary school teachers, so we're unable to see if there's been a substantial increase in qualified teachers ahead of 2030.

Goal #5

Achieve gender equality and empower all women and girls

Target 5.1

End all forms of discrimination against all women and girls everywhere

- Indicator 5.1.1: Whether or not legal frameworks are in place to promote, enforce and monitor equality and non-discrimination on the basis of sex

Target 5.1 introduces us to the work of UN Women, the UN body charged with the task of achieving gender equality, a key pillar of development. The advancement of women has been a focus of the UN since the UN Decade for Women from 1975-85, and for 68 annual sessions (as of 2024) the UN Women's Commission on the Status of Women have met to advance women's empowerment and gender equality.

To put such legal frameworks into effect, countries need to promote the adoption of laws affecting the life of women, and enforce them, covering the topics of violence against women, employment, marriage and family.

Article 1 of the Convention on the Elimination of All Forms of Discrimination Against Women (CEDAW) defines discrimination against women as:

"...any distinction, exclusion or restriction made on the basis of sex which has the effect or purpose of impairing or nullifying the recognition, enjoyment or exercise by women, irrespective of their marital status, on a basis of equality of men and women..."

All countries are States Parties to the CEDAW, except the US, Iran, Sudan, Somalia, Palau (which is in free association with the US), and Tonga.

Worldwide, as of 2022, 70% of countries have a legal framework addressing gender equality.[74] 79% have legal frameworks addressing violence against women.[75] 76% have legal frameworks addressing gender equality related to employment and economic benefits, and 80% of countries have legal frameworks addressing gender in relation to marriage and family.[76]

Given how broad the Target is, it's unlikely all forms of discrimination against all women and girls everywhere will be met by the end of the SDG period. It is feasible this could be achieved by the measure of legal frameworks, or adoption of CEDAW, even if not by enforcement of individual acts of human behaviour.

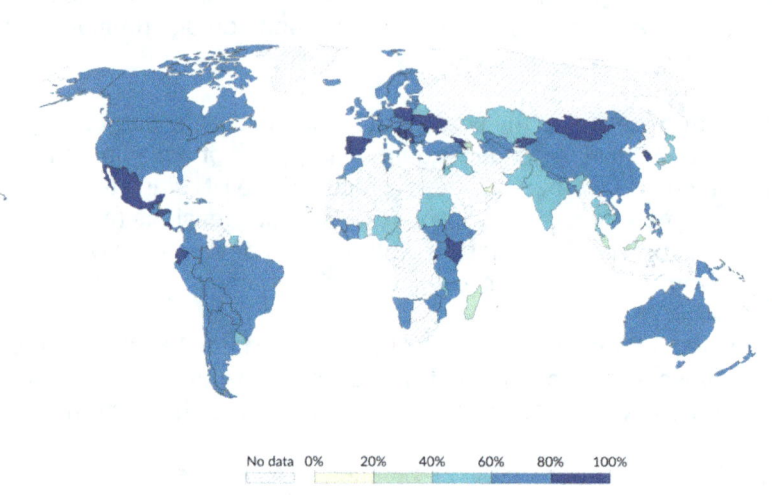

Target 5.2

Eliminate all forms of violence against all women and girls in the public and private spheres, including trafficking and sexual and other types of exploitation

- Indicator 5.2.1: Proportion of ever-partnered women and girls aged 15 years and older subjected to physical, sexual or psychological violence by a current or former intimate partner in the previous 12 months, by form of violence and by age
- Indicator 5.2.2: Proportion of women and girls aged 15 years and older subjected to sexual violence by persons other than an intimate partner in the previous 12 months, by age and place of occurrence

Violence against women is not only a crime in many countries, but violates human rights laws agreed upon at the international level in treaties. Looked at from a public health perspective, the threat it poses to the health of a population is of pandemic proportions. Such violence can be physical, sexual, or psychological.

The following human rights agreements are relevant to this topic:

- Declaration on the Elimination of Violence against Women, adopted by the UN General Assembly in 1993.
- Universal Declaration of Human Rights. The Declaration is international law for those who signed and ratified it via two treaties, adopted by the UN General Assembly in 1966:

- International Covenant on Civil and Political Rights. All but 20 countries are state parties.[77] Those who've not acted include South Sudan, Saudi Arabia, Oman, UAE, Bhutan, Malaysia and Myanmar. China has signed but not ratified.
- International Covenant on Economic, Social and Cultural Rights. The US is the main holdout from becoming a state party, having signed, but not ratified. Saudi Arabia, the same Gulf states as above, and Malaysia and Myanmar again haven't signed. Botswana, Mozambique, and about 20 other smaller countries haven't signed or ratified.
- Convention against Torture and Other Cruel, Inhuman or Degrading Treatment or Punishment. The General Assembly adopted this treaty in 1984. The largest country which isn't a state-party is India, which has signed, but not ratified. Other non-signatories include Bangladesh, Eswatini, Iran, Myanmar, Malaysia and Papua New Guinea.

On the path to elimination, 10% of women over 15-years-old worldwide experienced physical or sexual violence from an intimate partner in the past 12 months, as of 2018.[78] The highest proportions were in Democratic Republic of Congo and Afghanistan, both reporting above 30%.

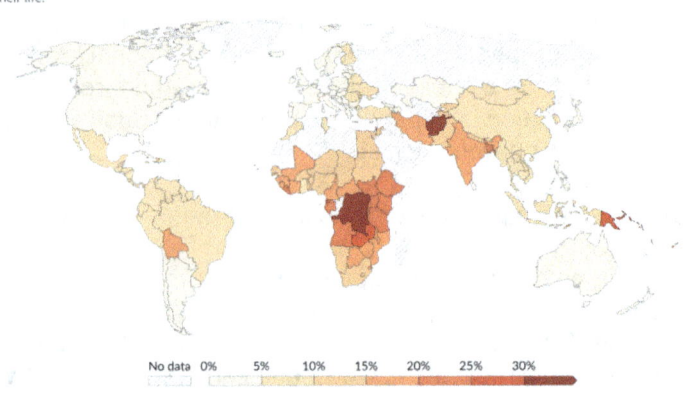

Share of women who experienced violence from an intimate partner, 2018

Ever-partnered women aged over 15 years who have been subject to physical or sexual violence by a current or former intimate partner in the last 12 months. An ever-partnered woman is a woman who has had an intimate partner at any time in their life.

Data source: Data from multiple sources compiled by the UN
OurWorldinData.org/women-rights | CC BY

Target 5.3

Eliminate all harmful practices, such as child, early and forced marriage and female genital mutilation

- Indicator 5.3.1: Proportion of women aged 20–24 years who were married or in a union before age 15 and before age 18
- Indicator 5.3.2: Proportion of girls and women aged 15–49 years who have undergone female genital mutilation, by age

Child and forced marriages, and female genital mutilations, are human rights violations, and early marriage can rob girls of education potential.

The worldwide proportion of women married before age 15 was 4% as of 2023, putting elimination within reach.[79] We don't have global rates for women married under age 18, but among countries with data, the highest were in the neighbouring countries of Niger, Chad and Central African Republic (60-76%), far from elimination.

Unpleasant as it may to be to discuss, imagine how much worse it could be to experience female genital mutilation, of which 230 million females do worldwide, often girls under 18.[80]

UN agencies have collaborated to present the statement entitled *Eliminating female genital mutilation*, approaching the topic from the perspectives of:

- health
- human rights

- development
- social and cultural practices
- children's rights
- women's rights
- reproductive rights

The countries with rates of female genital mutilation greater than 80% of the female population as of 2022, and are far off track to eliminate the practice, include:

- Mali
- Guinea
- Sierra Leone
- Egypt
- Sudan
- Djibouti
- Somalia (99% rate)[81]

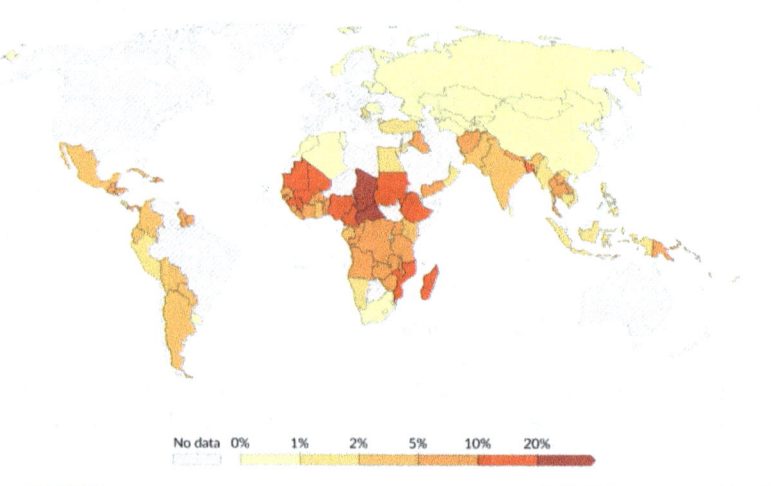

Share of women who were married by age 15, 2023
Women aged 20-24, who were married or in a union before they reached the age of 15.

Data source: UNICEF
OurWorldinData.org/women-rights | CC BY

Target 5.4

Recognize and value unpaid care and domestic work through the provision of public services, infrastructure and social protection policies and the promotion of shared responsibility within the household and the family as nationally appropriate

- Indicator 5.4.1: Proportion of time spent on unpaid domestic and care work, by sex, age and location

Unemployed individuals, or those performing unpaid work, are seldom recognised for their contribution, underutilised in the use of their time from an economic and social perspective - of relevance when considering gender across the globe.

Of the countries with data, the biggest disparity between the sexes in time spent on unpaid work was Mexico, where in 2022, Mexican men spent 11% of their time each day on unpaid work, and women 27%.[82]

Indicator 5.4.1 asks us to disaggregate the data by location. To separate Mexico's 2019 data, 31% of the time of rural women was unpaid work, compared to 27% for urban women, 10% for rural men, and 11% for urban men.[83]

Target 5.5

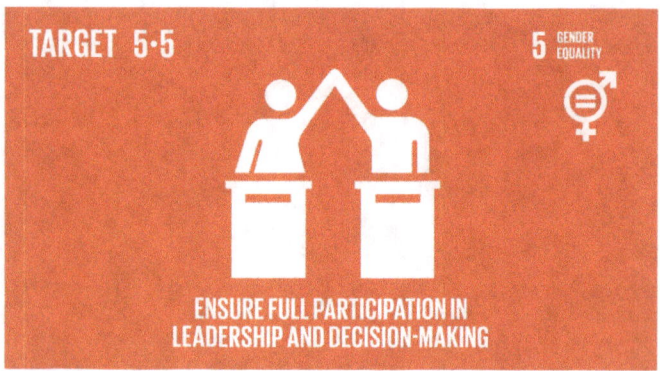

Ensure women's full and effective participation and equal opportunities for leadership at all levels of decision-making in political, economic and public life

- Indicator 5.5.1: Proportion of seats held by women in (a) national parliaments and (b) local governments
- Indicator 5.5.2: Proportion of women in managerial positions

Indicator 5.5.1 introduces us to the work of the Inter-Parliamentary Union (IPU), which is independent of, but works with the UN. Indicator 5.5.1 splits into two levels of governance: national parliaments and local governments. For the countries with data, UN Women reports 3 million women elected to local government.[84]

As of 2023, the global share of women in parliamentary seats is 26%, with the most in Rwanda (61%).[85] In local government, the global figure is 35%, the largest share in Antigua and Barbuda.[86]

Indicator 5.5.2 measures what share of women have a managerial occupation. Of the countries with data as of 2023, Jordan has the largest share of women in senior and middle management positions (57%).[87] The worldwide share of organisations with a female top manager is 18%.[88] Thailand had the greatest share among countries with data (64%).

Target 5.6

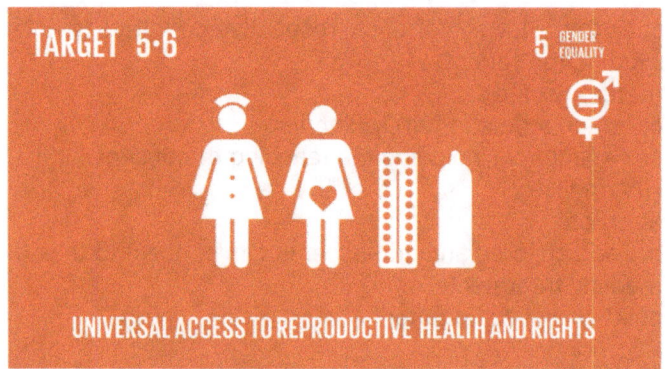

Ensure universal access to sexual and reproductive health and reproductive rights as agreed in accordance with the Programme of Action of the International Conference on Population and Development and the Beijing Platform for Action and the outcome documents of their review conferences

- Indicator 5.6.1: Proportion of women aged 15–49 years who make their own informed decisions regarding sexual relations, contraceptive use and reproductive health care
- Indicator 5.6.2: Number of countries with laws and regulations that guarantee full and equal access to women and men aged 15 years and older to sexual and reproductive health care, information and education

For women worldwide, who is making the decision about their own healthcare? Do women have the choice to use contraceptives, and can they refuse sex with a partner by the laws of the country they live in?

Fertility rates are highest in the least developed countries, but so is child mortality, which can result in families choosing to have more children to compensate. Women in such regions can have choices deprived of them around their reproductive decisions, but development allows women to delay childbirth, reducing fertility rates.

Target #5.6 mentions the International Conference on Population and Development, a 1994 UNFPA conference which addressed the pressures of population, fertility, and development. The Programme of Action, adopted at the ICPD, highlighted the issue of women's rights to their own decision-making in relation to sex and reproduction.

This extends to the laws in effect in respective countries upholding such rights, including matters of:
- maternity care
- contraception and family planning
- sex education, including the teaching of consent
- HIV and HPV
- abortion
- the age children and adolescents can consent to their own medical treatment
- child sexual exploitation

Target 5.6 mentions the Beijing Declaration and Platform of Action, a landmark guidance for intergovernmental progress in advancing gender equality, adopted in Beijing in 1995.

56% of women worldwide make their own informed decisions about sexual relations and contraceptive use.[89] The lowest rates are in sub-Saharan Africa, where only 38% of women face such choices, far from universal access.

76% of countries have laws as of 2022, ensuring the right to access sexual and reproductive health care for both sexes - not on track for universal access.[90]

Target 5.A

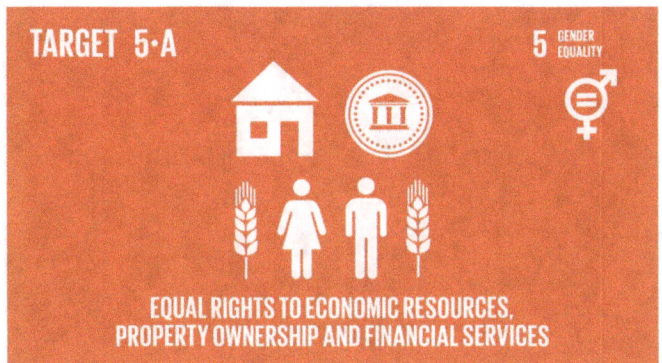

Undertake reforms to give women equal rights to economic resources, as well as access to ownership and control over land and other forms of property, financial services, inheritance and natural resources, in accordance with national laws

- Indicator 5.a.1: (a) Proportion of total agricultural population with ownership or secure rights over agricultural land, by sex; and (b) share of women among owners or rights-bearers of agricultural land, by type of tenure
- Indicator 5.a.2: Proportion of countries where the legal framework (including customary law) guarantees women's equal rights to land ownership and/or control

Among the countries with data for Indicator 5.a.1 as of 2023, most are developing countries. Cambodia leads, with 82% of women having secure agricultural land rights, and 54% of agricultural landowners were women.[91] Malawi had the largest share (57%), and Pakistan the least among those with data (2%).

Indicator 5.a.2 measures gender equality of land ownership rights enshrined in law. Among countries with data as of 2023, the highest guarantees of women's land ownership were in Colombia, Rwanda, Cambodia, Burkina Faso, Ethiopia and Lithuania.[92]

Target 5.B

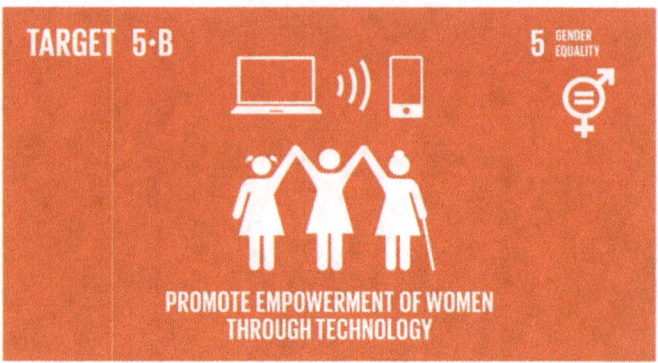

Enhance the use of enabling technology, in particular information and communications technology, to promote the empowerment of women

- Indicator 5.b.1: Proportion of individuals who own a mobile telephone, by sex

As of 2023, 74% of women own a mobile phone, an increase from 69% in 2015.[93] Among countries with data, 100% of women in Saudi Arabia, Bahrain and UAE have mobiles (with many countries' rates greater than 95%), and only 11% of women in Burundi.

Target 5.C

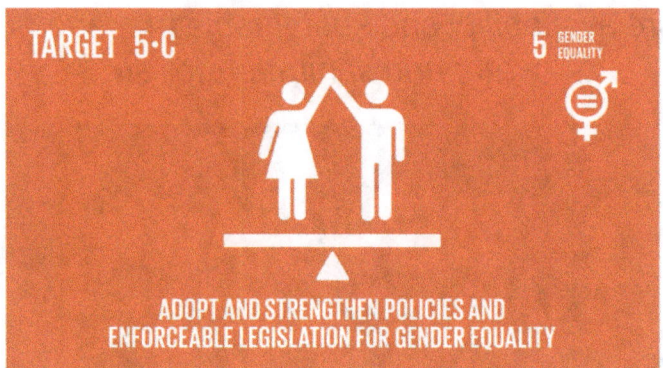

Adopt and strengthen sound policies and enforceable legislation for the promotion of gender equality and the empowerment of all women and girls at all levels

- Indicator 5.c.1: Proportion of countries with systems to track and make public allocations for gender equality and women's empowerment

Are national governments putting gender equality and women's empowerment into law? Has the government developed a national gender equality plan? Are governments held accountable by the populace to instil equality? Is an office or ministry of the government given a budget to spend on policies in favour of women, such as education? If a government hasn't budgeted for it, can it claim women's development to be a priority?

As of 2021, the global proportion of countries with systems to track public expenditure on gender equality stands at 26%.[94]

Goal #6

Ensure availability and sustainable management of water and sanitation for all

Target 6.1

By 2030, achieve universal and equitable access to safe and affordable drinking water for all

- Indicator 6.1.1: Proportion of population using safely managed drinking water services

Access to safe water is essential to health and disease prevention, and is a human right, though one deprived of 2.2 billion people, which now requires a six-fold acceleration of efforts to meet Target 6.1 by 2030.[95]

SDG #6 introduces us to UN Water, which coordinates the efforts of other UN agencies on the topic of water and sanitation.

Worldwide access to safe drinking water as of 2022 was 73%, off track for universal access by 2030.[96] The Central African Republic had the lowest access among countries with data, with only 6%.

Gaps of access are often due to where one lives - worldwide, 81% of the urban population have access, but only 62% for those living in rural locations.[97]

Target 6.2

By 2030, achieve access to adequate and equitable sanitation and hygiene for all and end open defecation, paying special attention to the needs of women and girls and those in vulnerable situations

- Indicator 6.2.1: Proportion of population using (a) safely managed sanitation services and (b) a handwashing facility with soap and water

The definition of a 'safely managed sanitation service' separates waste from human contact, is not shared with another household, and either disposes of the waste on-site, or removes and treats it off-site.

The lowest levels of safely managed sanitation facilities were in Sub-Saharan Africa, Yemen and Colombia, where less than a quarter of the population used safely managed sanitation services. The lowest levels of handwashing facilities were all in Sub-Saharan Africa countries.

The worldwide proportion of people with access to sanitation facilities was 56% as of 2022, and 75% for handwashing facilities, again off-track to provide sanitation and hygiene access to all by 2030, and end open defecation.[98]

Target 6.3

By 2030, improve water quality by reducing pollution, eliminating dumping and minimising release of hazardous chemicals and materials, halving the proportion of untreated wastewater and substantially increasing recycling and safe reuse globally

- Indicator 6.3.1: Proportion of domestic and industrial wastewater flows safely treated
- Indicator 6.3.2: Proportion of bodies of water with good ambient water quality

The proportion of treated domestic wastewater worldwide stands at 58% as of 2022, a mild increase since 2020, the only other data point to observe improvements in water quality in the SDG period.[99] Very few countries have enough data to report treatment for industrial wastewater.

The global proportion of water bodies with good water quality stands at 56% as of 2023, with no earlier data to see if there's been an improvement.[100]

Target 6.3's official UN Indicators only measure the end result of water quality, but not the means to get there. For example, there isn't an indicator to measure reductions of pollution, the elimination of dumping, the release of hazardous chemicals and materials, or recycling and reuse.

Target 6.4

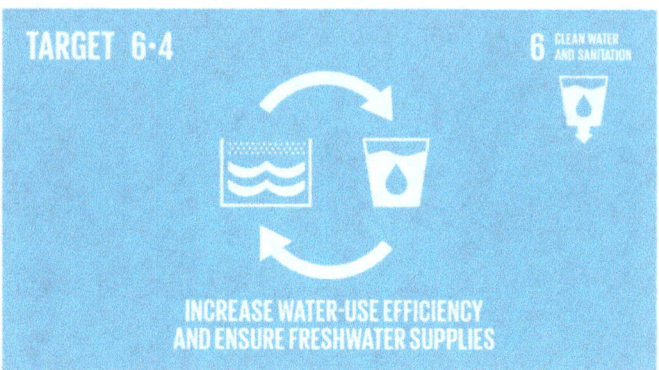

By 2030, substantially increase water-use efficiency across all sectors and ensure sustainable withdrawals and supply of freshwater to address water scarcity and substantially reduce the number of people suffering from water scarcity

- Indicator 6.4.1: Change in water-use efficiency over time
- Indicator 6.4.2: Level of water stress: freshwater withdrawal as a proportion of available freshwater resources

The activities which call upon water resources include the immense requirements of agriculture and resource extraction, manufacturing and construction, power supply, sewerage and waste treatment, and domestic water supply.

Water use efficiency is a measure in monetary terms, denominated in US dollars per cubic metre, calculated at the country level by dividing GDP by the number of cubic metres of freshwater withdrawn.

Worldwide, water efficiency in 2020 was $21 per cubic metre, an increase since 2015 from $19.29, though the target doesn't define how substantial an increase is necessary, nor is there data to disaggregate if the efficiency has been across all sectors.[101] The tiny country of Luxembourg was the most water efficient ($1,379 per cubic metre), and Madagascar the least ($0.91/m^3).[102]

We become at risk of water stress when withdrawing freshwater at a rate faster than it can renew, minus what the environment needs. As of 2021, there was 42 billion cubic metres of renewable water in the world, with an annual freshwater withdrawal rate of 3.9 billion cubic metres.[103]

We can calculate this to tell us how water stressed a country is by taking the amount of freshwater withdrawn (measured in cubic metres), divide this by the total renewable freshwater, and subtract the environment's requirements. After multiplying by 100, this gives us a percentage of water stress, which if greater than 75%, is considered high, affecting the drinking water supply, various economic sectors, and threatening food security.

Measured at the global level, the level of water stress is 18% as of 2021, unchanged since 2015, although Target 6.4 has asked us to reduce those living with water scarcity by 2030.[104]

Some countries even have a critical water stress greater than 100%, which occurs when withdrawing freshwater at a faster rate than the renewable sources can replenish. These countries span the Sahara, across the Mideast to Central Asia. Kuwait's water efficiency is a stratospheric 3,850%, followed by 1,587% in UAE, and 974% in Saudi Arabia.[105] Not only has Kuwait not decreased its water scarcity, it's doubled since 2000.

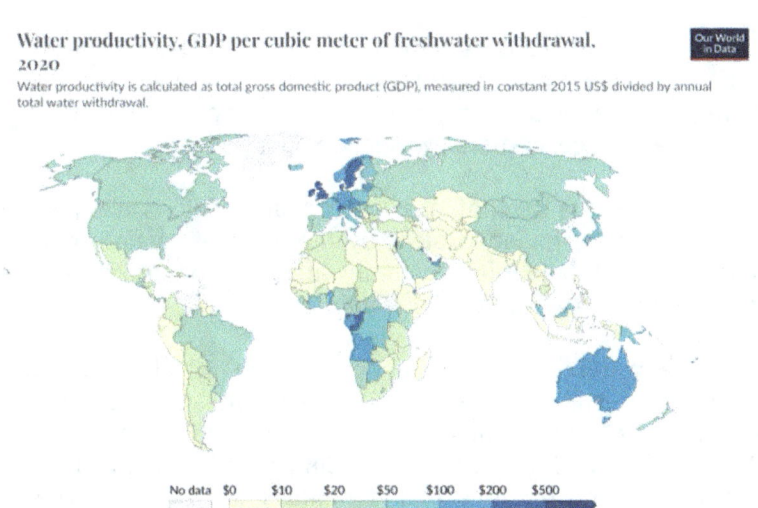

Target 6.5

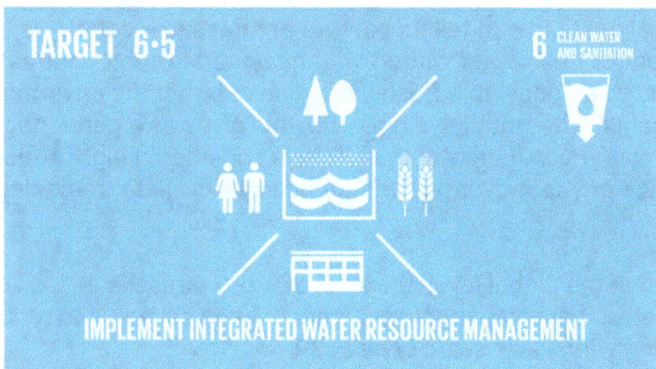

By 2030, implement integrated water resources management at all levels, including through transboundary cooperation as appropriate

- Indicator 6.5.1: Degree of integrated water resources management
- Indicator 6.5.2: Proportion of transboundary basin area with an operational arrangement for water cooperation

Managing water resources has large social and economic implications in water scarce regions, not only at the national level, but across countries within regions sharing a common border, whether a shared water body visible on the surface, or groundwater in an aquifer.

This topic seems ripe for conflict in water scarce regions, and competing interests need to be managed, aided by international treaties on the sustainable use of transboundary freshwater, the most prominent example being the 1997 Water Convention.

An integrated water resources management plan - which considers water from economic, social and environmental perspectives - is in effect across 57% of countries worldwide as of 2023, far off track to meet Target 6.5 by 2030.[106] France and Singapore lead with 100% implementation, and Timor-Leste and Papua New Guinea the lowest, with less than 20%. 46% of global aquifers had transboundary basins with arrangements to cooperate over water as of 2023, 66% in the case of river and lake basins, and 58% for both combined.[107]

Target 6.6

By 2020, protect and restore water-related ecosystems, including mountains, forests, wetlands, rivers, aquifers and lakes

- Indicator 6.6.1: Change in the extent of water-related ecosystems over time

This target introduces us to the Ramsar Convention on Wetlands, agreed to in Ramsar, Iran, in 1971.

Such is the nature of some types of wetlands, such as a fen, they've taken millennia to form, and once damaged, cannot be restored with ease. The Ramsar Convention categorises wetlands into three types: on the coast in marine environments, inland, and human-made, and lists those wetlands which have international importance.

A report taking stock of the state of the world's wetlands in 2015 deemed 45% degraded, losing 87% since the start of the 20th century.[108] Among the costs we bear for this are the loss of regulating services which wetland areas offer.

Though 2020 has passed, as of 2022, lakes and rivers cover 0.02% of the world's land, a number we want to maintain or increase for the purposes of Target 6.6.[109] Global wetlands coverage was 4% as of 2017, though it's the only year with data, so we're unable to see if these have been protected or restored in the SDG period.[110]

Target 6.A

By 2030, expand international cooperation and capacity-building support to developing countries in water- and sanitation-related activities and programmes, including water harvesting, desalination, water efficiency, wastewater treatment, recycling and reuse technologies

- Indicator 6.a.1: Amount of water- and sanitation-related official development assistance that is part of a government-coordinated spending plan

As of 2022, from ODA earmarked by the donor for water and sanitation, the biggest spenders on water in their respective government budgets were Egypt ($426 million), India ($356 million), Jordan (followed by Vietnam ($413 million).[111]

For the least developed countries, ODA received for water and sanitation was $2.8 billion, which rose in 2019 to $3.56 billion, but has since dropped back to $2.8 billion in 2022.[112]

Target 6.B

Support and strengthen the participation of local communities in improving water and sanitation management

- Indicator 6.b.1: Proportion of local administrative units with established and operational policies and procedures for participation of local communities in water and sanitation management

Target 6.b focuses on water at the local government level. A handy tool to assess policies is the OECD's Water Governance Indicator Framework, part of the OECD's water program, which recommends water policies to governments, including its 12 Principles on Water Governance.

As of 2022, 86% of countries had in place policies and procedures for community participation in water and sanitation, though earlier data isn't available to see if participation has been strengthened.[113]

Goal #7

Ensure access to affordable, reliable, sustainable and modern energy for all.

Target 7.1

By 2030, ensure universal access to affordable, reliable and modern energy services

- Indicator 7.1.1: Proportion of population with access to electricity
- Indicator 7.1.2: Proportion of population with primary reliance on clean fuels and technology

Electricity access is a marker of living standards and a necessity for health. Access to electricity worldwide was 91% as of 2021, leaving universal access by 2030 within reach.[114]

Europe and Central Asia have full electrification, as do the high-income and the upper-middle income countries. The regions of the Middle East and North Africa, Latin America and the Caribbean, and East Asia and the Pacific, have 97-98% coverage. The lower-middle income countries have a similar proportion to the global population, and 45% in low-income countries have electricity.

As we saw in Target 3.9, air pollution from stoves burning solid cooking fuels in households in some developing countries is a health risk, affects the environment, and contributes to climate change.

Access to clean cooking fuels was 71% of the world population as of 2021, off track for universal access by 2030.[115]

Target 7.2

By 2030, ensure universal access to affordable, reliable and modern energy services

- Indicator 7.2.1: Renewable energy share in the total final energy consumption

The renewable energy share of final energy consumption worldwide was 19% as of 2021 - far from this Target's aim of sustainable energy for all by 2030.[116] Two countries had a renewable energy share higher than 95%: Democratic Republic of Congo and Somalia, which is positive, as of 675 million people without lighting in the world, four out of 5 live in Sub-Saharan Africa.[117] These and others above 90% were all among the poorest countries in the world.

While a third of electricity worldwide was generated from renewable energy powering electricity as of 2020, it powered a tenth for heating, and a few percent for transport.[118]

Target 7.3

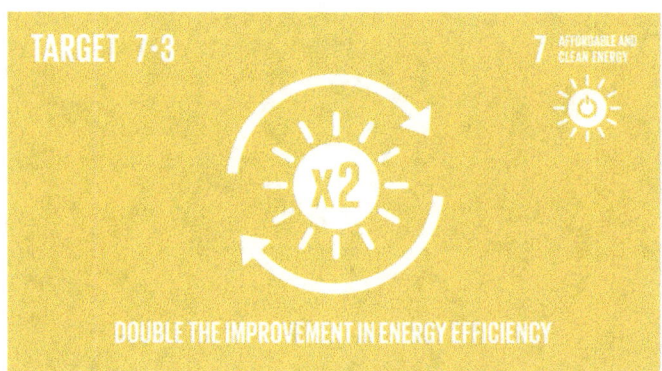

By 2030, double the global rate of improvement in energy efficiency

- Indicator 7.3.1: Energy intensity measured in terms of primary energy and GDP

Energy efficiency is the amount of energy needed to produce a unit of economic output, or energy expended per dollar in the economy, and efforts to improve energy efficiency are a key pillar of decarbonisation and ensuring sustainable energy for all.

Global energy intensity in 2020 was $4.54 of economic value produced per megajoule of energy used, down a little from the adoption of the SDGs in 2015 of $4.83 per megajoule.[119] The International Energy Agency specifies the baseline period as 1990-2010 compared to 2010-2030, aiming to increase the annual improvement in global energy efficiency to 2.6% over the latter span.[120] As it's been off-track from doubling through to 2019, the rate now needs to be 3.2% by 2030, although instead of measuring this, Target 7.3's sole indicator measures energy intensity of GDP.

Target 7.A

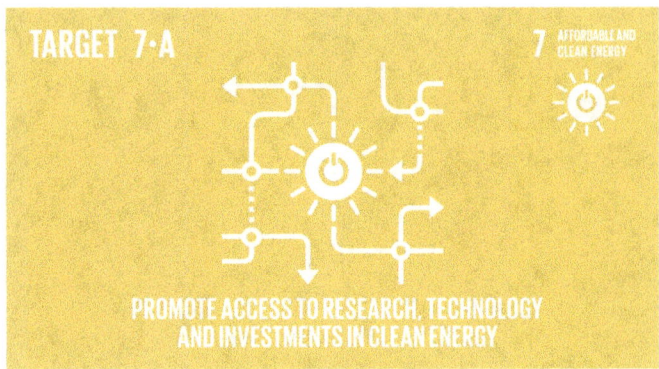

By 2030, enhance international cooperation to facilitate access to clean energy research and technology, including renewable energy, energy efficiency and advanced and cleaner fossil-fuel technology, and promote investment in energy infrastructure and clean energy technology

- Indicator 7.a.1: International financial flows to developing countries in support of clean energy research and development and renewable energy production, including in hybrid systems

The International Renewable Energy Agency tracks development flows from high-income countries for renewable energy. In 2022, donor countries gave $15 billion as foreign aid intended for clean energy - down from the 2016 peak of $23 billion, but still up a couple billion since 2015.[121] If this is able to be maintained through to 2030, this Target can be met, as flows will have been enhanced, even though there's been an annual decline since 2017.

Brazil and South Africa received the most in 2022, both over $1.2 billion.

Target 7.B

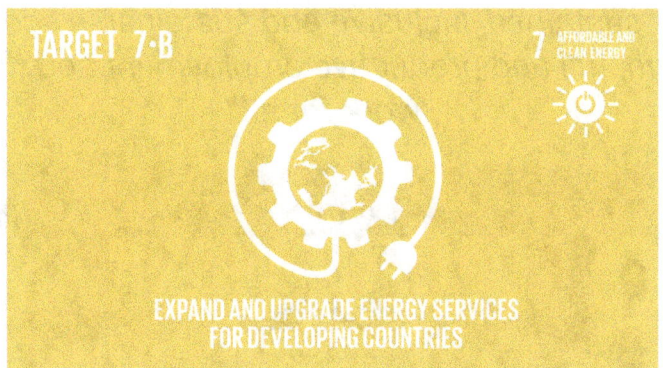

By 2030, expand infrastructure and upgrade technology for supplying modern and sustainable energy services for all in developing countries, in particular least developed countries, small island developing States and landlocked developing countries, in accordance with their respective programmes of support

- Indicator 7.b.1: Installed renewable energy-generating capacity in developing and developed countries (in watts per capita)

The least developed countries face the prospect of the largest growth in population in the years to come, so their existing dearth of energy takes on an extra importance for their eventual access to be derived from renewable sources.

If not, and energy access comes from fossil fuels, the fight against climate change would be all but lost to accommodate the increase in living standards. All countries have a right to develop, so it's vital access comes via renewable energy.

The global capacity of renewable energy as of 2022 was 424 watts per capita, an increase from 154 watts per capita in 2015.[122] In the least developed countries, it was 39 watts per capita, up from 28 watts in 2015. In the Small Island Developing States, renewable energy capacity was 101 watts per capita, up from 55 watts in 2015. As long as these increases stay in place, the 2030 aim of expanding sustainable energy infrastructure will be met.

Goal #8

Foster sustained, inclusive and sustainable economic growth, full and productive employment and decent work for all.

Target 8.1

Sustain per capita economic growth in accordance with national circumstances and, in particular, at least 7 per cent gross domestic product growth per annum in the least developed countries

- Indicator 8.1.1: Annual growth rate of real GDP per capita

For GDP growth to be sustained, it must keep pace with price rises from inflation and population growth i.e. if GDP rises 7%, but so does population growth, the actual rise in GDP cancels out, and if the GDP grows 7%, but the inflation rate is 4%, then GDP growth is only 3%.

The per capita annual growth rate for the world economy in 2022 was 2.28%, an increase from 1.86% in 2015.[123] In the years following 2015, there was a dip in 2016 to 1.60%, followed by an increase in 2017, a tiny dip in 2018, a drop in 2019 to 1.51%, then a big drop in 2020 to -4.03%. 2021 saw a 5.31% rise, before halving in 2022.

In 2022, the only least developed country with GDP growth rates above 7% was Niger (7.4%).[124]

Target 8.2

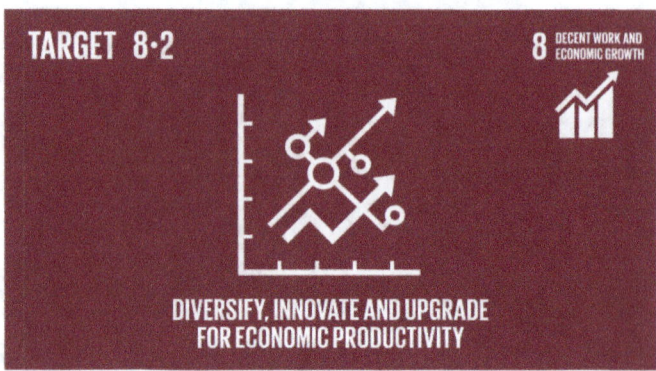

Achieve higher levels of economic productivity through diversification, technological upgrading and innovation, including through a focus on high-value added and labour-intensive sectors

- Indicator 8.2.1: Annual growth rate of real GDP per employed person

Employment is a fundamental marker of development and the healthy functioning of a society, but since the adoption of the SDGs, growth hasn't been as promising as hoped. Diversification of an economy may be necessary in those countries reliant on exports of natural resources, which may suffer from the "resource curse," when a country underperforms after neglecting its non-resource economic sectors.

One of the SDSN's proposed indicators to measure the technological and innovation aspect of Target 8.2 is an index of a country's broadband speed, bandwidth and affordability.

The GDP growth rate per employed person worldwide as of 2023 was 0.3%, down from the 2015 rate of 2%.[125] Between this span, there was a large drop in 2020 of -0.3%, which recovered to the earlier levels around 2%, before dropping again. Given this trend of economic productivity, levels aren't higher than at the start of the SDG period, off-track for Target 8.2.

Target 8.3

Promote development-oriented policies that support productive activities, decent job creation, entrepreneurship, creativity and innovation, and encourage the formalisation and growth of micro-, small- and medium-sized enterprises, including through access to financial services

- Indicator 8.3.1: Proportion of informal employment in total employment, by sector and sex

Of the countries with data as of 2023, many of the least developed countries had greater than 80% of workers in non-agricultural informal work.[126] The number of workers in the informal sector are also high in the very populous countries of India (81%) and Bangladesh (91%).

Much fewer countries have data for informal employment in the agriculture sector. Many of those missing data have the highest proportions of informality in non-agricultural jobs. Developing countries with 2023 data had between 80-100% informal employment in agriculture.[127]

Jordan has the greatest gender imbalance in the non-agricultural sector among countries with data. 53% of Jordanian men were in informal employment, and 32% of females.[128] In agriculture, the biggest gender disparities among countries with data were in Serbia, where 31% of males, compared to 68% of women, were in informal employment, and Poland (42% of males and 78% of women).

Target 8.4

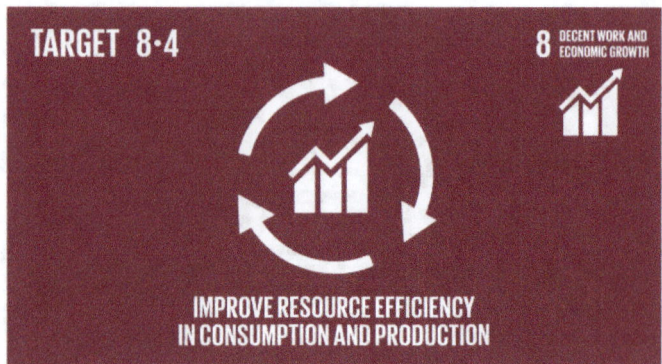

Improve progressively, through 2030, global resource efficiency in consumption and production and endeavour to decouple economic growth from environmental degradation, in accordance with the 10-Year Framework of Programmes on Sustainable Consumption and Production, with developed countries taking the lead

- Indicator 8.4.1: Material Footprint, material footprint per capita, and material footprint per GDP
- Indicator 8.4.2: Domestic material consumption, domestic material consumption per capita, and domestic material consumption per GDP

Material footprint is a measure of the tonnage of natural resources extracted from the Earth, including metal ores, fossil fuels, minerals, or living matter from plants and animals, many of which are finite.

By contrast, the concept of domestic material consumption is a measure of materials used within a country.

The economy - the basis upon which we all prosper - rests upon a foundation of the environment. How do we live on a planet with a spiking increase in resource use? What is the pathway out of this pattern, to unlink economic growth from scarce resource use and extraction?

The world's material footprint per capita was 12 tonnes as of 2022, the same as 2015, with no improvement.[129]

The world's material footprint in 2022 was 1kg per US dollar of GDP, with not much of a change since 2015.[130]

Target 8.4 asks developed countries to take the lead. As a proxy for the developed countries, Europe and Northern America used 400 grams per US dollar of domestic material consumption in 2022.[131] Northern America used 26 tonnes of material per capita, and Europe 12 tonnes, little changed since 2015.[132]

Domestic material consumption per capita, 2022

Domestic material consumption reports the amount of materials used in a national economy. It is the sum of materials extracted domestically and the amount of direct imports, with the amount of exports subtracted.

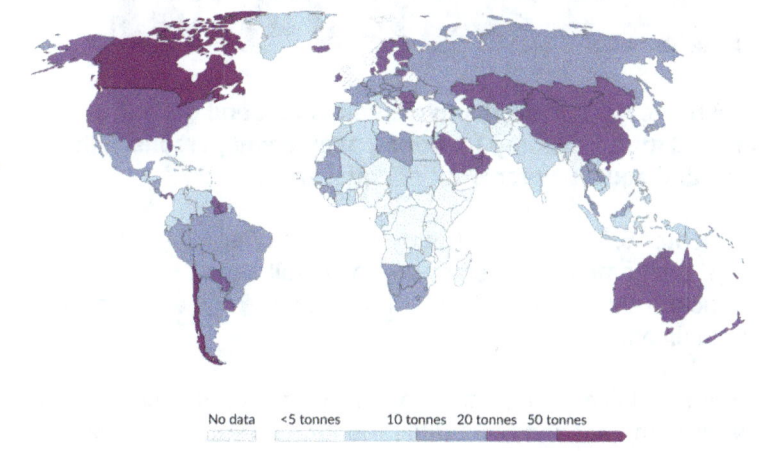

No data   <5 tonnes   10 tonnes   20 tonnes   50 tonnes

Data source: United Nations Environment Programme   OurWorldinData.org/sdgs/economic-growth | CC BY

Target 8.5

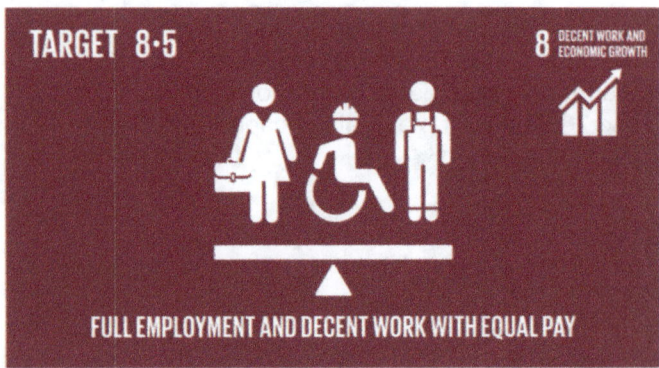

By 2030, achieve full and productive employment and decent work for all women and men, including for young people and persons with disabilities, and equal pay for work of equal value

- Indicator 8.5.1: Average hourly earnings of employees, by sex, age, occupation and persons with disabilities
- Indicator 8.5.2: Unemployment rate, by sex, age and persons with disabilities

Article 23 of the Universal Declaration of Human Rights enshrines the right to work, with "just and favourable" conditions and remuneration, to ensure an "existence worthy of human dignity", as well as equal pay for equal work.

Only a couple dozen countries have data for employees' average hourly earnings. By sex, the greatest difference was in South Korea, where the average hourly earnings of male employees were $23.96, and $15.91 for women.[133]

The global unemployment rate as of 2022 was 5.3%, with fractional gender differences, but would need to reduce to 0% to meet full employment by 2030.[134] Country-level data exists for unemployment rates for persons with disabilities, but not by age.

Target 8.6

By 2020, substantially reduce the proportion of youth not in employment, education or training

- Indicator 8.6.1: Proportion of youth (aged 15–24 years) not in education, employment or training

As of 2023, 21% of young people were not in education, employment or training (NEET) worldwide, the same as in 2015.[135] Young women are twice as likely as young men to not be in employment, education or training.[136]

By 2020, there had been a couple percent increase of youth NEET since 2015, meaning Target 8.6's aim to reduce the proportion of youth NEET by 2020 was missed.

Of the countries with data for Indicator 8.6.1, Niger and Afghanistan performed worst, with 68%, and the Netherlands led with 3% in 2022.[137]

Target 8.7

Take immediate and effective measures to eradicate forced labour, end modern slavery and human trafficking and secure the prohibition and elimination of the worst forms of child labour, including recruitment and use of child soldiers, and by 2025 end child labour in all its forms

- Indicator 8.7.1: Proportion and number of children aged 5–17 years engaged in child labour, by sex and age

At the time of writing, in the first couple days of 2025, we haven't ended child labour, so this facet of the Target is already foregone. As of 2020, UNICEF estimated 160 million children worldwide were in child labour, an increase of 8.4 million in the preceding four years.[138] As of 2021, there were an estimated 50 million modern slaves, 27 million of these in forced labour, far off track to end modern slavery.[139]

Target 8.7 encapsulates measures taken to eradicate forced labour via UN labour and human rights agreements:

- International Labour Standards
- Convention on the Rights of the Child
- Declaration on the Protection of Women and Children in Emergency and Armed Conflict
- ILO Declaration on Fundamental Principles and Rights at Work
- ILO Forced Labour Convention
- Slavery Convention
- Worst Forms of Child Labour Convention

Among those with data as of 2023, the countries with more than a third of children engaged in labour were Burkina Faso, Cameroon, Togo, and Chad.[140] The biggest gender gap among countries with 2023 data was Senegal, with 8% of girls in labour, and a quarter of boys.[141]

Share of children engaged in labor, 2023

Child employment (for children aged 5-17 years) is defined based on the amount of time spent participating in economic activities. The threshold for being engaged in labor varies by age group: for ages 5-11, it is one hour; for ages 12-14, it is 14 hours; and for ages 15-17, it is 43 hours.

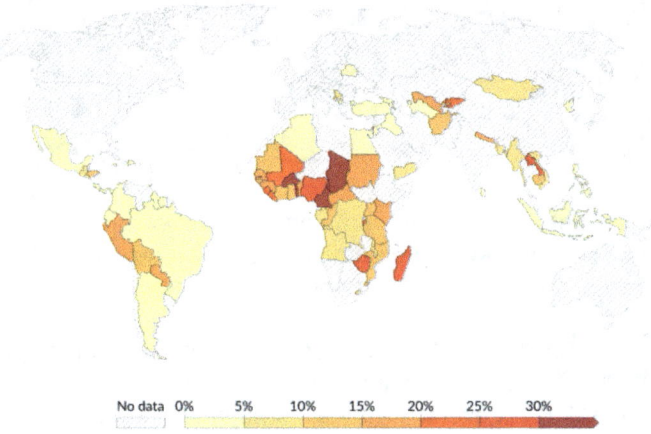

Data source: UNICEF and International Labour Organization
OurWorldinData.org/violence-against-rights-for-children | CC BY

Target 8.8

Protect labour rights and promote safe and secure working environments for all workers, including migrant workers, in particular women migrants, and those in precarious employment

- Indicator 8.8.1: Fatal and non-fatal occupational injuries per 100,000 workers, by sex and migrant status
- Indicator 8.8.2: Level of national compliance with labour rights (freedom of association and collective bargaining) based on International Labour Organization (ILO) textual sources and national legislation, by sex and migrant status

We need work to be safe and secure to achieve the other Goals relating to poverty reduction, with decent work helping to fulfil the equality aspirations of the SDGs. Precarious employment refers to work which, by contrast, is inferior in its compensation, job security and hours of work. Precarious work may feel like the only option for women who've migrated to escape poverty, conflict or climate change, sometimes facing gender-based and sexual violence on the job in a foreign country, which may not even afford them a livelihood.

We earlier explored two treaties which put the Universal Declaration of Human Rights into effect. One of these, the International Covenant on Civil and Political Rights, enshrines freedom of association into international law for its parties in Article 22:

"Everyone shall have the right to freedom of association with others, including the right to form and join trade unions for the protection of his interests."

Some of the International Labour Organization conventions which guide international labour law include:

- Freedom of Association and Protection of the Right to Organise Convention of 1948
- Abolition of Forced Labour Convention of 1957
- Protection of Wages Convention of 1949
- Right to Organise and Collective Bargaining Convention of 1949
- Discrimination (Employment and Occupation) Convention of 1958
- Migration for Employment Convention of 1949
- Migrant Workers (Supplementary Provisions) Convention of 1975
- Domestic Workers Convention of 2011

Relevant human rights instruments adopted by the UN General Assembly include:

- International Convention on the Elimination of All Forms of Racial Discrimination
- International Convention on the Protection of the Rights of All Migrant Workers and Members of Their Families

Also relevant are two protocols supplementing a UN convention against transnational organized crime:

- Protocol to Prevent, Suppress and Punish Trafficking in Persons Especially Women and Children of 2000
- Protocol Against the Smuggling of Migrants by Land, Sea and Air

Many of the countries which may have been at highest risk of fatal occupational injuries don't have data as of 2021, though among those who do, the highest was Egypt, with 10 per 100,000 workers.[142] For non-fatal occupational injuries, the highest was Costa Rica, with 9,421 per 100,000 workers as of 2022.[143] When measuring the level of national compliance with labour rights, the world has scored 4.8 on a 0-10 scale as of 2022, with 0 the best.[144] The worst performers as of 2022 were Iran and UAE, with a score of 10.[145]

Target 8.9

By 2030, devise and implement policies to promote sustainable tourism that creates jobs and promotes local culture and products

- Indicator 8.9.1: Tourism direct GDP as a proportion of total GDP and in growth rate

Sustainable tourism are practices in a destination conducive with the three pillars of sustainable development i.e. economic development, social inclusion for the local communities and their culture, and protection of the natural environment.

Target 8.9 introduces the work of another of the UN agencies, UN Tourism. Rather than measuring policies or jobs in the tourism sector, Indicator 8.9.1 measures tourism direct GDP, the value added by all industries contributing to tourism. The world leaders among countries with data as of 2022 are Antigua and Barbuda and Fiji, both with a little more than 10% of GDP.[146]

Target 8.10

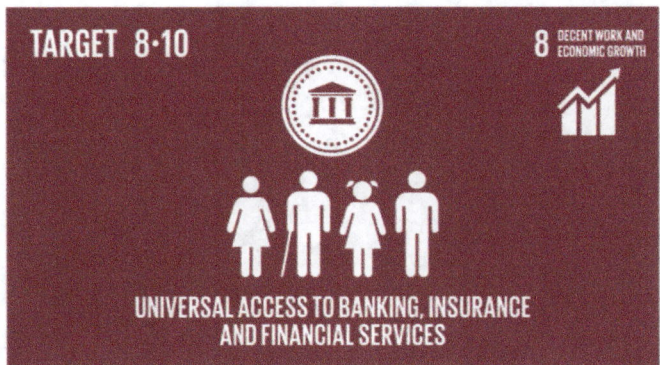

Strengthen the capacity of domestic financial institutions to encourage and expand access to banking, insurance and financial services for all

- Indicator 8.10.1: (a) Number of commercial bank branches per 100,000 adults and (b) Number of automated teller machines (ATMs) per 100,000 adults
- Indicator 8.10.2: Proportion of adults (15 years and older) with an account at a bank or other financial institution or with a mobile-money-service provider

Financial inclusion has become much more accessible with the proliferation of digital payments, giving those living in remote community's access to financial institutions, and to transact, via telecommunications.

Worldwide, the number of commercial bank branches per 100,000 adults was 11.2 as of 2021, about the same as 2015.[147] For the same year, there were 39 ATMs per 100,000 people worldwide, a slight increase from 36 in 2015.[148]

The proportion of adults with a bank account or similar in 2021 was 76%, an increase since the Goals' adoption of 62%, though still distant from achieving financial services for all.[149]

Target 8.A

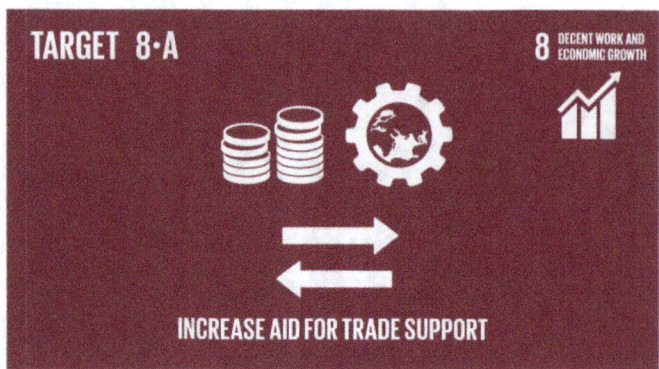

Increase Aid for Trade support for developing countries, in particular least developed countries, including through the Enhanced Integrated Framework for Trade-related Technical Assistance to Least Developed Countries

- Indicator 8.a.1: Aid for Trade commitments and disbursements

Aid for Trade is an initiative of the OECD and WTO for high-income donor countries to help developing countries, as is the Enhanced Integrated Framework. An example of aid which might help towards improving a country's ability to trade is infrastructure, such as transport and utilities networks.

For the high-income OECD countries which give development aid, we can separate what they've given as intended for Aid for Trade. Based on this, the developing regions received $52.5 billion as Aid for Trade in 2021, a figure which has gone up and down in the years since the adoption of the Goals in 2015, when it was $62 billion.[150]

In 2022, least developed countries received $19 billion in Aid for Trade commitments - the same as 2015, though varying year-on-year since, missing the aim of Target 8.a to increase Aid for Trade support.

On the donor side, the largest 2022 commitments earmarked for Air for Trade came from Japan, which gave $10 billion, and Germany ($8 billion).[151]

Target 8.B

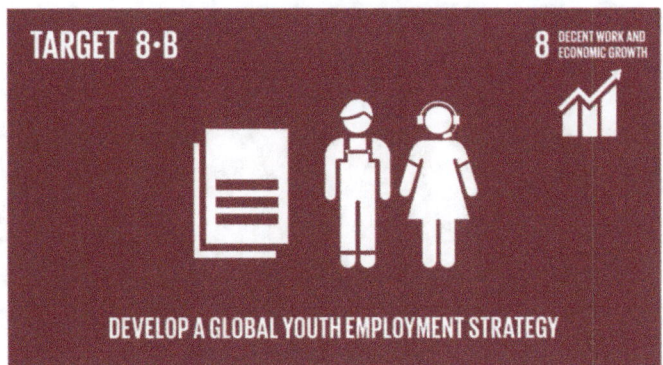

By 2020, develop and operationalize a global strategy for youth employment and implement the Global Jobs Pact of the International Labour Organization

- Indicator 8.b.1: Existence of a developed and operationalized national strategy for youth employment, as a distinct strategy or as part of a national employment strategy

As of 2020, a global strategy to address the one in four young people not working or in formal training wasn't developed, and rather than measuring implementation of the ILO's Global Jobs Pact adopted in 2009, Indicator 8.b.1 measures national youth employment strategies.

Among these one in four young people, some never would have worked, have given up looking, whereas others may be in insecure jobs in the informal sector, leading to long-term effects on those from already poverty-stricken backgrounds.

Target 8.b looks at whether each country has implemented legislation and policies intended to create jobs for youth, which a large swath of countries have as of 2022.[152]

Goal #9

Build resilient infrastructure, promote inclusive and sustainable industrialization and foster innovation

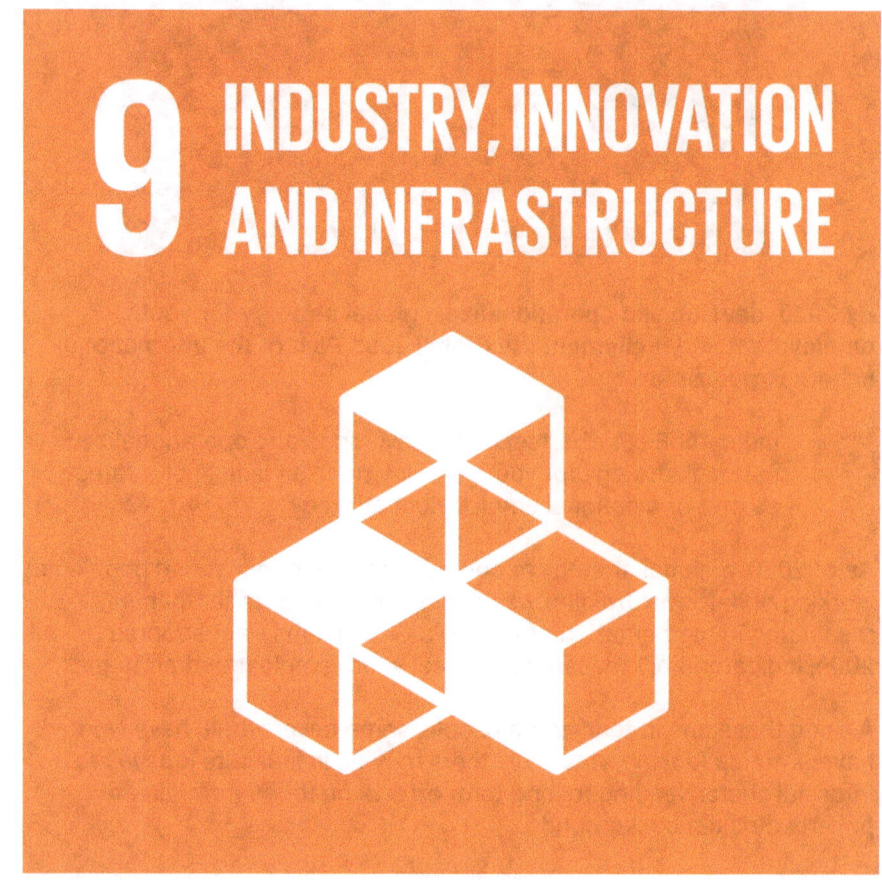

Target 9.1

Develop quality, reliable, sustainable and resilient infrastructure, including regional and transborder infrastructure, to support economic development and human well-being, with a focus on affordable and equitable access for all

- Indicator 9.1.1: Proportion of the rural population who live within 2 km of an all-season road
- Indicator 9.1.2: Passenger and freight volumes, by mode of transport

It's crucial for countries to have transport networks to foster trade and economic development, but infrastructure needs to encourage sustainable transport i.e. to be accessible and decarbonised, whether land-based, maritime or aviation.

Less than 20% of the rural populations of Madagascar, Zambia, Lesotho, and the United Arab Emirates lived within 2 kilometres of an all-season road as of 2021.[153]

The leader in passenger transport by rail is China, with passengers travelling 975 billion kilometres in 2021.[154] By aviation, the US was the leader, with 1.53 trillion km of a global total of 5.89 billion kilometres in 2022.[155] Measuring air freight by tonnes of kilometres flown, the US (46 billion) and China (21 billion) again lead in 2021, out of a worldwide total of 219 billion.[156]

Target 9.2

Promote inclusive and sustainable industrialization and, by 2030, significantly raise industry's share of employment and gross domestic product, in line with national circumstances, and double its share in least developed countries

- Indicator 9.2.1: Manufacturing value added as a proportion of GDP and per capita
- Indicator 9.2.2: Manufacturing employment as a proportion of total employment

The more an economy develops, the further it tends to move away from manufacturing toward services. The least developed countries have a high proportion of primary industry i.e. agriculture, forestry, fishing, and resource extraction, which offer less value added.

Manufacturing value added is the dollar value of all manufacturing output, minus any inputs. The 2022 world leader, as a proportion of GDP, was Ireland (38%), followed by Algeria (35%).[157] Manufacturing as a proportion of gross world product was 16% in 2022, the same since 2015.

Target 9.2 aims for manufacturing to double by 2030 in the least developed countries. As a proxy for the least developed countries, manufacturing was 11% of the share of GDP in Sub-Saharan Africa, up only 1% since the adoption of the Goals. In South Asia, manufacturing was 14% of the region's GDP, a 1% decrease since 2015.

The leader in manufacturing as a share of all employment was China, consisting of 29% of all jobs as of 2020, followed by Czechia with 26% in 2022.[158] The worldwide share in 2022 was 14%, about the same since the adoption of the Goals.[159] For the least developed countries, the share was 8%, again unchanged since 2015, off track for a substantial increase by 2030.

Share of manufacturing in gross domestic product (GDP), 2022

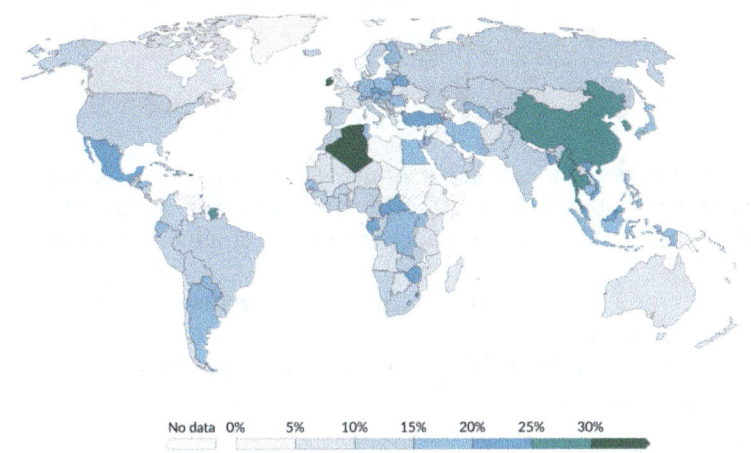

Manufacturing comprises units engaged in the physical, or chemical transformation of materials, substances, or components into new products.

Data source: Multiple sources compiled by World Bank (2024)

OurWorldinData.org/economic-growth | CC BY

Target 9.3

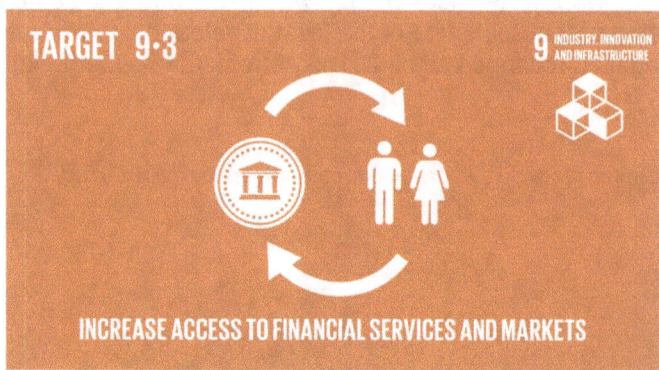

Increase the access of small-scale industrial and other enterprises, in particular in developing countries, to financial services, including affordable credit, and their integration into value chains and markets

- Indicator 9.3.1: Proportion of small-scale industries in total industry value added
- Indicator 9.3.2: Proportion of small-scale industries with a loan or line of credit

The leader in share of small-scale industries among total manufacturing as of 2020 was Cyprus (31%).[160] Although Target 9.3 focuses on developing countries, most African countries and many others don't have data for Indicator 9.3.1.

For this Target's second measure of small-scale industries with a loan or credit, the 2023 world share was 30%, and 17% for the least developed countries, though there isn't earlier data to see if there's been an increase since the adoption of the SDGs.[161]

Target 9.4

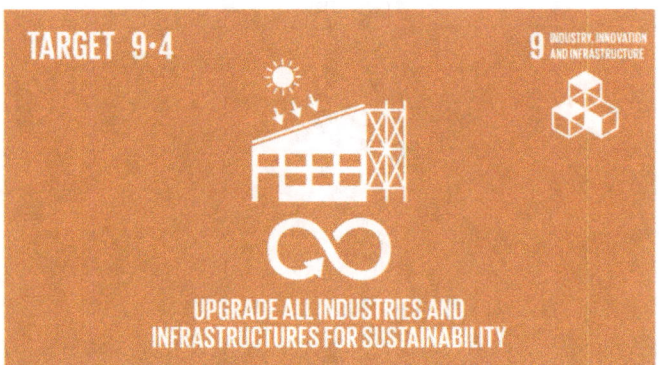

By 2030, upgrade infrastructure and retrofit industries to make them sustainable, with increased resource-use efficiency and greater adoption of clean and environmentally sound technologies and industrial processes, with all countries taking action in accordance with their respective capabilities

- Indicator 9.4.1: CO2 emission per unit of value added

As of 2022, the world emits 290 grams of carbon dioxide per dollar of value added in the manufacturing sector, unchanged since the most recent data around the adoption of the SDGs, suggesting efforts to upgrade infrastructure and retrofit clean technologies are stagnating on the road to 2030.[162] The country with the most emissions per dollar of manufacturing value added was North Korea (1.39kg).

CO2 emissions from energy were at a record high in 2022.[163]

Target 9.5

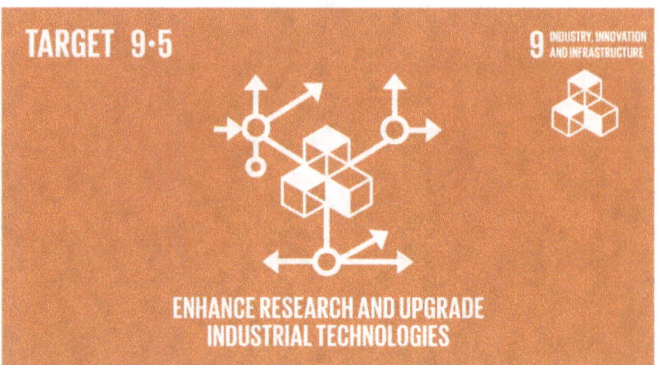

Enhance scientific research, upgrade the technological capabilities of industrial sectors in all countries, in particular developing countries, including, by 2030, encouraging innovation and substantially increasing the number of research and development workers per 1 million people and public and private research and development spending

- Indicator 9.5.1: Research and development expenditure as a proportion of GDP
- Indicator 9.5.2: Researchers (in full-time equivalent) per million inhabitants

Innovations in science and technology allow industries to grow, and countries to develop. One of the clearest measures of innovation is R&D expenditure as a percentage of GDP. The largest R&D spenders are the high-income countries and China, but for the sake of Target 9.5, we want the developing countries to foster science and technology innovations.

Spending on R&D as a share of global world product was 2.7% as of 2021, rising a fractional amount since the start of the SDG period.[164] This was an impressive share, though still half of the leader, Israel (5.6%). The leaders for the measure of researchers in a country's population comports with R&D expenditure. The worldwide total as of 2021 was 1,525 researchers per million people, a slight increase since 2015 from 1,385 per million.[165] The world leader as of 2021 was South Korea, with 9,082 researchers per million in the population, but Korea's competitor for world leader in research, Israel, didn't have 2021 data for comparison.

Target 9.A

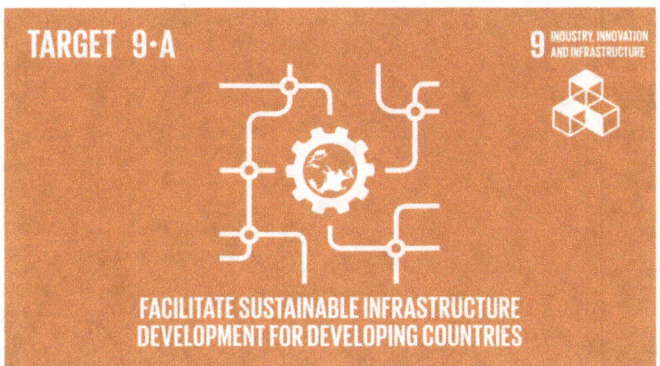

Facilitate sustainable and resilient infrastructure development in developing countries through enhanced financial, technological and technical support to African countries, least developed countries, landlocked developing countries and small island developing States

- Indicator 9.a.1: Total official international support (official development assistance plus other official flows) to infrastructure

The biggest recipient country for aid earmarked to be spent on infrastructure as of 2022 was India, which received $8 billion.[166] In Africa, it was $16 billion, $13 billion for the least developed countries, and $1.7 billion for small island states.

Target 9.B

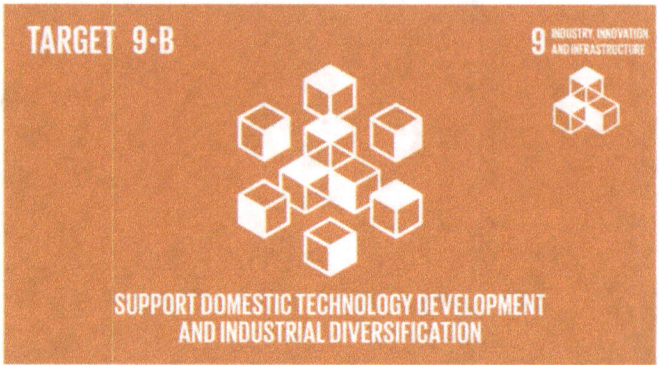

Support domestic technology development, research and innovation in developing countries, including by ensuring a conducive policy environment for, inter alia, industrial diversification and value addition to commodities

- Indicator 9.b.1: Proportion of medium and high-tech industry value added in total value added

The value added from manufacturing in medium- and high-tech industries implies an elevated level of R&D expenditure.

As of 2021, the world leader by share of GDP from medium- and high-tech value added was Singapore (85%), followed by Switzerland (70%).[167] The world's share was 45%, unchanged since 2015, though there's insufficient data for developing countries.

Target 9.C

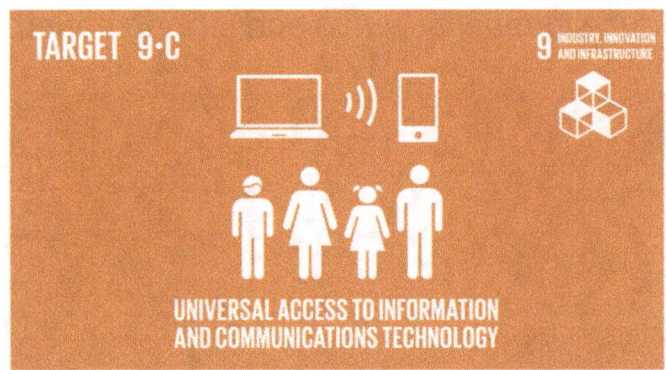

Significantly increase access to information and communications technology and strive to provide universal and affordable access to the Internet in least developed countries by 2020

- Indicator 9.c.1: Proportion of population covered by a mobile network, by technology

Mobile phone coverage is one of the brightest spots in SDG progress, although we still missed the aim of Target 9.c of universal access to the internet for least developed countries by 2020.

As of 2023, 98% of the global population had access to 2G networks, an increase of a couple percentage points since 2015.[168] 3G coverage was 95%, up from 78% in 2015, and 4G access was 90%, up from 43% in 2015. Among the least developed countries, there was 91% 2G access across the population, up from 86% in 2015. 4G access for the LDCs stood at 56% in 2023, up from 15%. In 2020, 91% of the population of LDCs had access to 2G networks, and 79% to 3G, short of the 100% access needed for universality.

Goal #10

Reduce inequality within and among countries

Target 10.1

By 2030, progressively achieve and sustain income growth of the bottom 40 per cent of the population at a rate higher than the national average

- Indicator 10.1.1: Growth rates of household expenditure or income per capita among the bottom 40 per cent of the population and the total population

SDG #10 serves as a symbol of one of the three pillars of sustainable development: social inclusion, to share prosperity across society, ensuring the alleviation of pockets of poverty not only across countries, but within.

Indicator 10.1.1 measures this via the growth rate of the income or consumption of the bottom 40% of the population by income.

The most impressive growth rate differential in income between the bottom 40%, and the entire population, was in Myanmar, which had a 2023 income growth rate for the bottom 40% of 9%, compared to 1% for the national average.[169]

Target 10.2

By 2030, empower and promote the social, economic and political inclusion of all, irrespective of age, sex, disability, race, ethnicity, origin, religion or economic or other status

- Indicator 10.2.1: Proportion of people living below 50 per cent of median income, by sex, age and persons with disabilities

A quarter of the global population lives below half the median income as of 2024, unchanged since 2015, equal to the worst performer (Honduras), suggesting inclusion of all by 2030 will be missed.[170]

Target 10.3

Ensure equal opportunity and reduce inequalities of outcome, including by eliminating discriminatory laws, policies and practices and promoting appropriate legislation, policies and action in this regard

- Indicator 10.3.1: Proportion of population reporting having personally felt discriminated against or harassed in the previous 12 months based on a ground of discrimination prohibited under international human rights law

Target 10.3 only has a subjective measure of discrimination, but not of each nation's equal opportunity laws and policies.

Only a couple dozen countries have data for Indicator 10.3.1 as of 2023.[171] Among these, the highest rates of discrimination were in Uganda, Tuvalu, Kiribati, and Estonia. In these countries, more than a third of the population felt discriminated against in the previous year.

By contrast, countries with rates below 5% include Vietnam, Cuba, and Belarus - the former two communist countries, and Belarus in transition from communism.

Target 10.4

Adopt policies, especially fiscal, wage and social protection policies, and progressively achieve greater equality

- Indicator 10.4.1: Labour share of GDP
- Indicator 10.4.2: Redistributive impact of fiscal policy

The biggest laggard of the labour share of GDP as of 2020 was Venezuela, with only 10% of the country's output going toward labour - the rest to capital.[172]

By contrast, the world's share of labour to gross world product is 54%, much the same since 2015, stagnant toward the aim of a progressive achievement of equality by this measure. The world leaders were Switzerland and Nigeria, both with 68% labour share.

Indicator 10.4.2 measures the impact of policies intended for redistribution of income before and after taxes via the Gini index. The higher the Gini index number, the more unequal a country in income. The leaders in progress for this measure are all European, which shouldn't be surprising, given the region has high tax rates. Some of these leading countries managed to reduce their 2020 Gini index by a third or more via taxation policies.[173] Among countries with data, none became less equal due to redistributive policies.

Target 10.5

Improve the regulation and monitoring of global financial markets and institutions and strengthen the implementation of such regulations

- Indicator 10.5.1: Financial Soundness Indicators

Calamities in financial markets are relevant to Goal #10. Although they may wipe out the assets of the rich in the largest volumes, they're likely to affect the poorest the most in living standards. Target 10.5 aims to stem the risk to the global economy from shocks, or otherwise build its resilience, trying to identify vulnerabilities in the system ahead of time. The measurement of this is the International Monetary Fund's Financial Soundness Indicators. An example of one of these Financial Soundness Indicators is the number or value of non-performing loans held by banks which are late in repayment, or unlikely to be repaid. A series of three agreements named after the Swiss city of Basel serve as rules for banks in relation to the assets they need to hold as a fraction of what they loan, intended to avert crises in the global financial system, as experienced in 2007-08. The Basel Committee on Banking Supervision is part of the Bank of International Settlements, which has international oversight of banks, and oversees these agreements. We'll look at the performance of the world's biggest financial market, the United States, which precipitated the crisis of 2007-08. Return on assets was 1.45% in 2021 compared to 0.22% in 2009, in the wake of the crisis. The amount of capital which banks must keep as a fraction of their lending was 8.62% in 2021, little different than in 2009. Non-performing loans were a 0.81% share of all loans in 2021, down from 5% in 2009.

Target 10.6

Ensure enhanced representation and voice for developing countries in decision-making in global international economic and financial institutions in order to deliver more effective, credible, accountable and legitimate institutions

- Indicator 10.6.1: Proportion of members and voting rights of developing countries in international organizations

The equality in representation which Target 10.6 aims for is reflective of Article 2 of the UN Charter, based on:

"...the principle of the sovereign equality of all its Members."

Indicator 10.6.1 measures representation of the least developing countries in the following international organisations:

- UN General Assembly
- UN Security Council
- UN Economic and Social Council
- International Monetary Fund
- World Bank Group
    - International Bank for Reconstruction and Development
    - International Finance Corporation
- African Development Bank
- Asian Development Bank
- Inter-American Development Bank
- World Trade Organisation

- Financial Stability Board

Earlier Targets have mentioned many of these institutions, except the regional development banks, which offer investment in their respective regions. The two institutes mentioned under the umbrella of the World Bank are due to the World Bank Group consisting of five organisations. The Financial Stability Board serves a similar purpose to the Basel Committee mentioned in the previous Target.

The share of membership of LDCs for most of these bodies has been the same throughout the SDG period, except the UN Security Council, of which the non-permanent seats rotate among nations, and the Inter-American Bank, which rose in 2022.

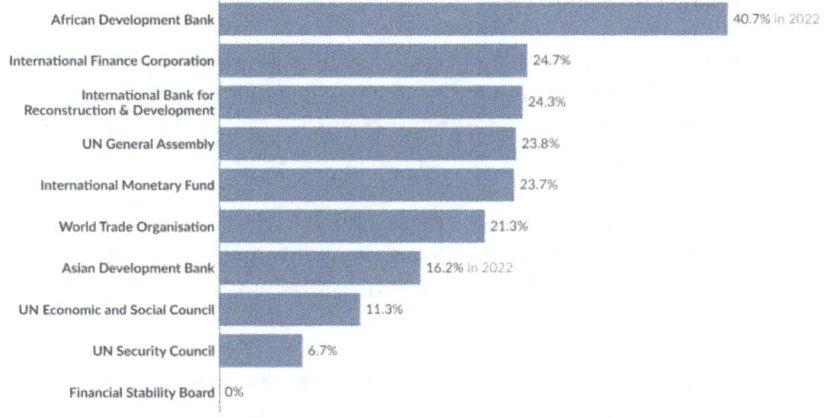

Target 10.7

Facilitate orderly, safe, regular and responsible migration and mobility of people, including through the implementation of planned and well-managed migration policies

- Indicator 10.7.1: Recruitment cost borne by employee as a proportion of monthly income earned in country of destination
- Indicator 10.7.2: Proportion of countries with migration policies that facilitate orderly, safe, regular and responsible migration and mobility of people
- Indicator 10.7.3: Number of people who died or disappeared in the process of migration towards an international destination
- Indicator 10.7.4: Proportion of the population who are refugees, by country of origin

Target 10.7's focus on migration introduces the work of the IOM, the UN's migration agency.

Target 10.7 measures outcomes, in contrast to the implementation of migration policies. There's inadequate data for Indicator 10.7.1 about the cost borne by a worker to find work abroad, though Bangladesh is one of the sole countries with data. For 2022, it cost Bangladeshis travelling abroad the equivalent of 17 months' pay to secure work.[174]

The IOM's Migration Governance Framework is relevant to Indicator 10.7.2, setting out principles to ensure "orderly, safe, regular and responsible migration." Only 62% countries have policies meeting this criterion as of 2021.[175]

Of relevance to Indicator 10.7.3 is the work of the Missing Migrants Project, which tracks deaths along international migratory routes. Since 2014, these deaths amounted to an estimated 70,938 (as of December 2024). In 2023, the Missing Migrants Project reported 8,177 migrants died or disappeared in such circumstances.[176]

The UNHCR (UN High Commissioner for Refugees) is the UN's refugee agency, which works in complement with the IOM to support the 117.3 million displaced refugees worldwide as of 2023.[177] The 1951 Refugee Convention guides the work of both UNHCR and IOM.

Per country of origin, in 2022, the highest concentration of refugees came from Venezuela, Central African Republic, South Sudan, Eritrea, Ukraine and Syria.

In each of these countries, between a tenth to a third of their respective populations had fled abroad as refugees.

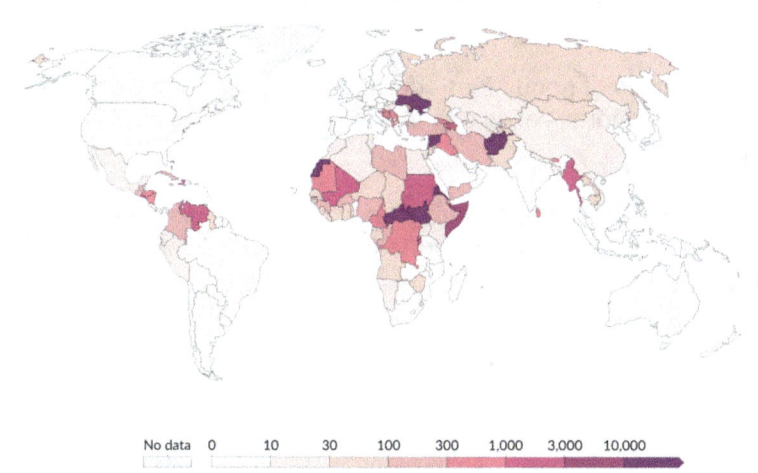

Number of refugees per 100,000 population, by country of origin, 2023
People recognized as refugees¹, as a proportion of the total population of their country of origin.

Data source: UNHCR (2024); Population based on various sources (2024)
OurWorldinData.org/migration | CC BY

Target 10.A

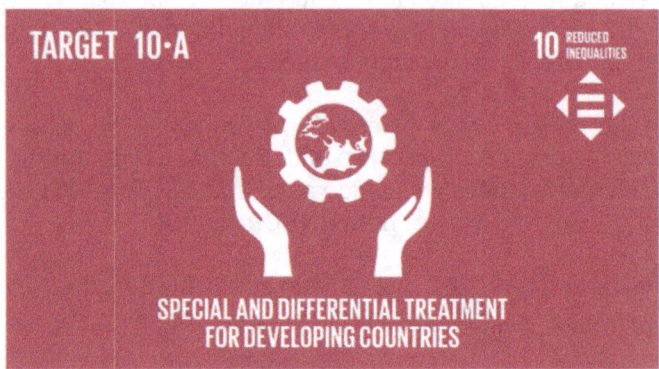

Implement the principle of special and differential treatment for developing countries, in particular least developed countries, in accordance with World Trade Organization agreements

- Indicator 10.a.1: Proportion of tariff lines applied to imports from least developed countries and developing countries with zero-tariff

In classifying types of goods for trade, some countries apply a separate code to certain imports, called a tariff line, which pose obstacles to trading partners.

Worldwide, the share of imports from least developed countries which the importing country waived all tariffs to zero was 62% as of 2022.[178]

Target 10.B

Encourage official development assistance and financial flows, including foreign direct investment, to States where the need is greatest, in particular least developed countries, African countries, small island developing States and landlocked developing countries, in accordance with their national plans and programmes

- Indicator 10.b.1: Total resource flows for development, by recipient and donor countries and type of flow (e.g. official development assistance, foreign direct investment and other flows)

The biggest recipients of development aid (including foreign direct investment) were China, India, Egypt, Brazil, and Mexico, which each received $10-30 billion in 2021.[179] This data isn't disaggregated by type of flow, to separate ODA, foreign direct investment, and other flows, nor is it grouped into LDCs, SIDS, and landlocked developing countries, where the need is greatest. The biggest donor government was the US, which was the leader by total sum, rather than as a proportion of their GDP.[180]

Target 10.C

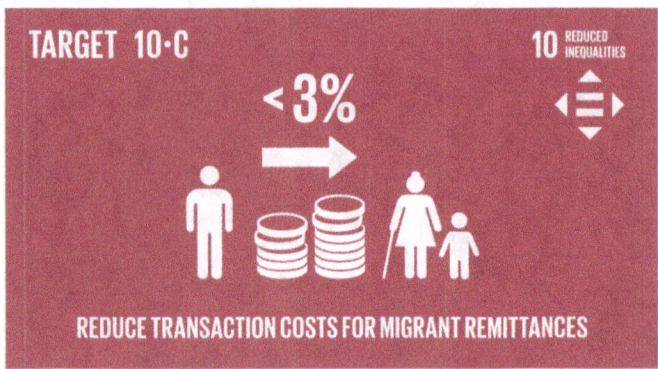

By 2030, reduce to less than 3 per cent the transaction costs of migrant remittances and eliminate remittance corridors with costs higher than 5 per cent

- Indicator 10.c.1: Remittance costs as a proportion of the amount remitted

Many countries don't have data for Indicator 10.c.1, though among those who do, Tanzania had the highest remittance costs as of 2021, equalling 28% of the value of the amount remitted, far from the 2030 aim of less than 3%.[181]

Goal #11

Make cities and human settlements inclusive, safe, resilient and sustainable

Target 11.1

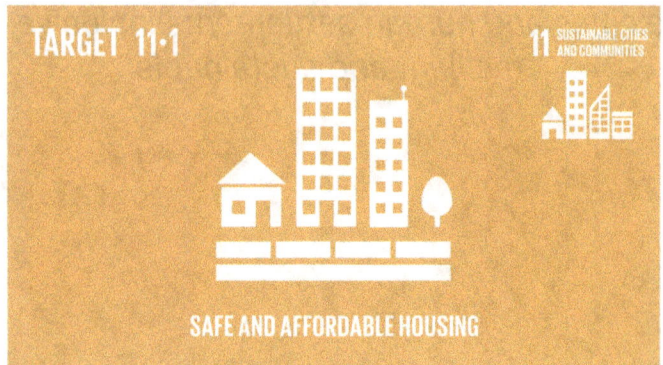

By 2030, ensure access for all to adequate, safe and affordable housing and basic services and upgrade slums

- Indicator 11.1.1: Proportion of urban population living in slums, informal settlements or inadequate housing

Target 11.1 of the Sustainable Development Goals carries on the work of Target 7.d of the Millennium Development Goals, which was to:

"Achieve, by 2020, a significant improvement in the lives of at least 100 million slum dwellers."

The world met Target 7.D of the MDGs threefold well before 2020, but the total number living in slums increased by 88 million over the MDG period between 2000-2015.[182]

UN-Habitat, also known as the UN Human Settlements Programme, is the UN agency with most relevance to SDG #11. Its efforts seek to uphold Article 25 of the Universal Declaration of Human Rights:

"Everyone has the right to a standard of living adequate for health and wellbeing."

An estimated 1.6 billion people live in inadequate housing, a billion of these in slums and informal settlements.[183]

The year following the adoption of the SDGs, the UN held a conference known as Habitat III, which adopted the New Urban Agenda, with a focus on sustainable cities.

As of 2022, a quarter of the global population live in slums, informal settlements, or inadequate housing.[184] Among countries with data, South Sudan had the highest concentration, with 94% of its population, followed by Mali, Burkina Faso, and Chad, each with more than 80%, far off track for access to all by 2030 of affordable and safe housing.

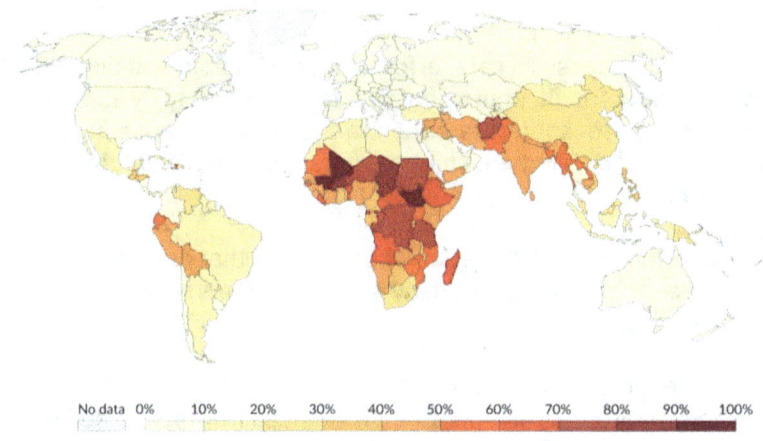

Target 11.2

By 2030, provide access to safe, affordable, accessible and sustainable transport systems for all, improving road safety, notably by expanding public transport, with special attention to the needs of those in vulnerable situations, women, children, persons with disabilities and older persons

- Indicator 11.2.1: Proportion of population that has convenient access to public transport, by sex, age and persons with disabilities

For public transport to be convenient, it must perform in adherence to the timetable and routes, and paratransit services may be needed in supplement to cater to those with special needs.

The countries of the European single market take the lead for Indicator 11.2.1, alongside Israel, New Zealand, and a handful of smaller states, which each had greater than 90% convenient access to public transport as of 2020.[185] Many countries are still far off track ahead of 2030, and we don't have disaggregated data for access for women, children, the disabled and the elderly. Those with less than 10% convenient access were Zambia, Iraq, Jordan, and the Solomon Islands.

Target 11.3

By 2030, enhance inclusive and sustainable urbanization and capacity for participatory, integrated and sustainable human settlement planning and management in all countries

- Indicator 11.3.1: Ratio of land consumption rate to population growth rate
- Indicator 11.3.2: Proportion of cities with a direct participation structure of civil society in urban planning and management that operates regularly and democratically

As populations grow, whether due to births or migration patterns, cities need to plan to accommodate these extra souls.

Although the UN has defined Indicators for this Target, countries haven't collected enough data for UN Habitat to measure progress toward 2030.

Target 11.4

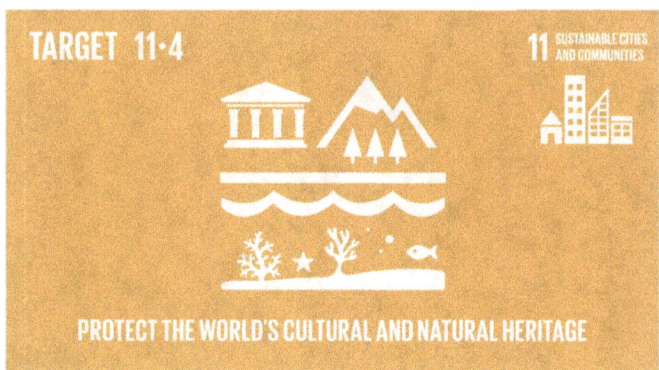

Strengthen efforts to protect and safeguard the world's cultural and natural heritage

- Indicator 11.4.1: Total per capita expenditure on the preservation, protection and conservation of all cultural and natural heritage, by source of funding (public, private), type of heritage (cultural, natural) and level of government (national, regional, and local/municipal)

Only a handful of countries have data for Indicator 11.4.1. Among those, countries spending over $100 per capita on cultural and natural heritage were:

- Luxembourg
- Sweden
- France
- Switzerland
- Czech Republic
- Finland
- Malta
- Denmark[186]

Target 11.5

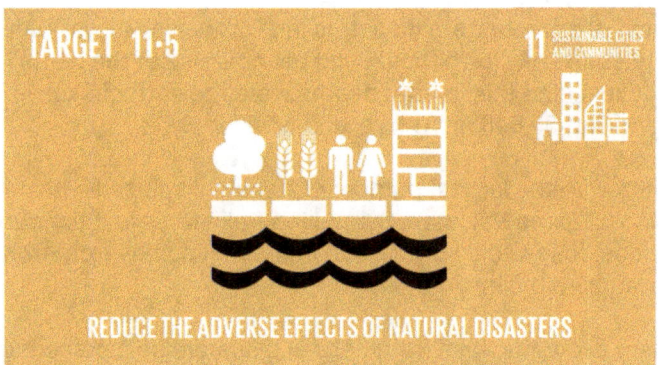

By 2030, significantly reduce the number of deaths and the number of people affected and substantially decrease the direct economic losses relative to global gross domestic product caused by disasters, including water-related disasters, with a focus on protecting the poor and people in vulnerable situations

- Indicator 11.5.1: Number of deaths, missing persons and directly affected persons attributed to disasters per 100,000 population
- Indicator 11.5.2: Direct economic loss attributed to disasters in relation to global gross domestic product (GDP)
- Indicator 11.5.3: (a) Damage to critical infrastructure and (b) number of disruptions to basic services, attributed to disasters

Even though we cannot control what Nature throws at us (other than mitigating climate change by decarbonising), we can employ resilience efforts to reduce losses of life and economic value in the face of disasters by 2030.

The total global number of people affected by natural disasters has varied each year since the adoption of the SDGs - the most in this span in 2016 (395 million), and the lowest in 2018 (74 million).[187] 2016 was the year in this period when the most people worldwide became homeless due to disasters, totalling 2.4 million.[188]

The year with the highest death rates from disasters in the SDG period was 2023 (1.08 per 100,000), and 2016 the least (0.1 per 100,000).[189]

2023 was the highest year for injuries from disasters in the SDG period, totalling 151,420.[190]

The highest death rate from disasters in 2023 was in Libya, with 179 per 100,000 because of Storm Daniel and the collapse of the dams in Derna.[191] Exceeding this in total deaths were the earthquakes in Türkiye and Syria, killing 50,840 in Türkiye, and 5,900 in Syria.

The country with the largest number of people displaced within its own borders in 2022 was Pakistan. 8.1 million Pakistanis lost their homes due to floods, followed by 5.5 million in the Philippines from tropical cyclones, and 3.6 million in China.[192]

The biggest economic loss from natural disasters as a percentage of GDP was in Somalia, which lost 5% of its economy's 2022 output.[193]

In the SDG period, 2017 was the year of biggest global economic losses to natural disasters as a proportion of the global economy, equal to 0.4% of gross world product.[194]

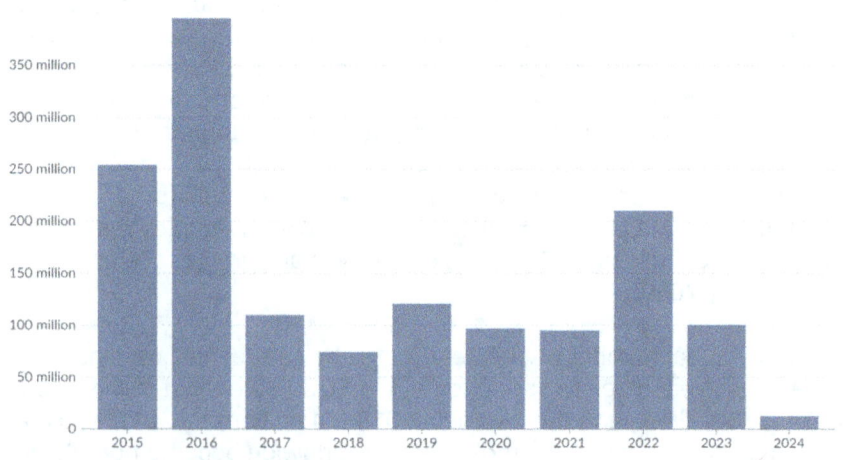

Target 11.6

By 2030, reduce the adverse per capita environmental impact of cities, including by paying special attention to air quality and municipal and other waste management

- Indicator 11.6.1: Proportion of municipal solid waste collected and managed in controlled facilities out of total municipal waste generated, by cities
- Indicator 11.6.2: Annual mean levels of fine particulate matter (e.g. PM2.5 and PM10) in cities (population weighted)

It's ideal if we can process waste in a materials recovery facility, which once recycled, are sold on, to be used as inputs to make new products. Other solutions include mechanical biological treatment, using the principles of composting or decomposition; and incineration, harnessing the resultant energy for re-use. Before all this though, it's best if we're able to prevent waste.

Very few countries reported data on the proportion of their municipalities with waste services, but all countries have data on the second Indicator of this Target.

As a measure of air quality, the 2019 global average exposure to particulate matter of 2.5 micrograms in diameter or less was 31 micrograms per cubic metre, a moderate reduction since 2015 of 35 micrograms.[195]

Target 11.7

By 2030, provide universal access to safe, inclusive and accessible, green and public spaces, in particular for women and children, older persons and persons with disabilities

- Indicator 11.7.1: Average share of the built-up area of cities that is open space for public use for all, by sex, age and persons with disabilities
- Indicator 11.7.2: Proportion of persons victim of non-sexual or sexual harassment, by sex, age, disability status and place of occurrence, in the previous 12 months

Indicator 11.7.2 recalls Target 5.2.

There's no international data available for Indicator 11.71 as of 2024. For Indicator 11.7.2, only a dismal six countries have data, so we're unable to track progress toward 2030 for universal access to safe and inclusive public spaces.

Target 11.A

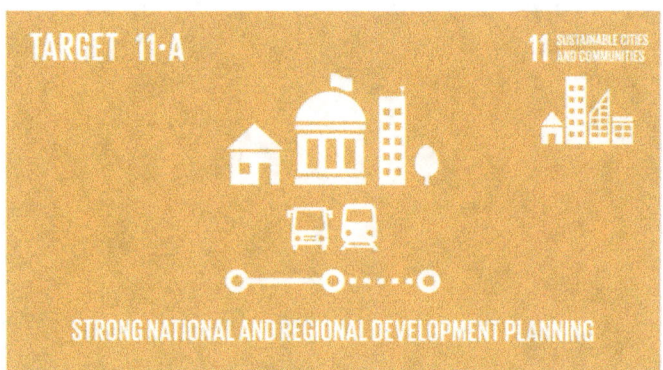

Support positive economic, social and environmental links between urban, peri-urban and rural areas by strengthening national and regional development planning

- Indicator 11.a.1: Number of countries that have national urban policies or regional development plans that (a) respond to population dynamics; (b) ensure balanced territorial development; and (c) increase local fiscal space

According to UN Habitat, a national urban policy promotes:

"...more transformative, productive, inclusive, and resilient urban development for the long term."

UN Habitat hosts the Urban Policy Platform, a knowledge base to help countries develop best practices to craft their urban policies.

As of 2020, neither the US nor Canada have national urban policies meeting the criteria of Target 11.a, though all but a handful of the rest of the Americas do.[196] All but a few African countries have such policies, as does Eurasia and Oceania, except North Macedonia, Azerbaijan, North Korea, Russia, and some microstates.

Target 11.B

By 2020, substantially increase the number of cities and human settlements adopting and implementing integrated policies and plans towards inclusion, resource efficiency, mitigation and adaptation to climate change, resilience to disasters, and develop and implement, in line with the Sendai Framework for Disaster Risk Reduction 2015–2030, holistic disaster risk management at all levels

- Indicator 11.b.1: Number of countries that adopt and implement national disaster risk reduction strategies in line with the Sendai Framework for Disaster Risk Reduction 2015–2030
- Indicator 11.b.2: Proportion of local governments that adopt and implement local disaster risk reduction strategies in line with national disaster risk reduction strategies

Neither of the Indicators for Target 11.b acknowledge the inclusion and resource efficiency policy aspects of the Target. We're here reintroduced to the Sendai Framework, covered earlier within Target 1.5.

As of 2023, many countries are without data for Indicator 11.b.1, so we're unable to measure whether Target 10.b was met by 2020, though most countries with data have made some progress.

The progress for Indicator 11.b.2, relating to local government disaster risk reduction, is a patchwork, with no identifiable patterns in the adoption of strategies across countries.

150

Target 11.C

Support least developed countries, including through financial and technical assistance, in building sustainable and resilient buildings utilizing local materials

It may seem incredulous, but with five years to spare in the SDG period, the UN hasn't developed an Indicator for this Target - an opportunity to introduce us to the concept of the classification of SDG Indicators into three tiers.

For one of the official UN Indicators to be Tier 1, the underlying concepts need to be clear; a method to measure needs to exist; and half of all countries must produce data with regularity.

Tier 2 Indicators meet the same criteria as Tier 1, except countries produce data less often.

For Tier 3 Indicators, the UN is still developing a method.

Goal #12

Ensure sustainable consumption and production patterns

Target 12.1

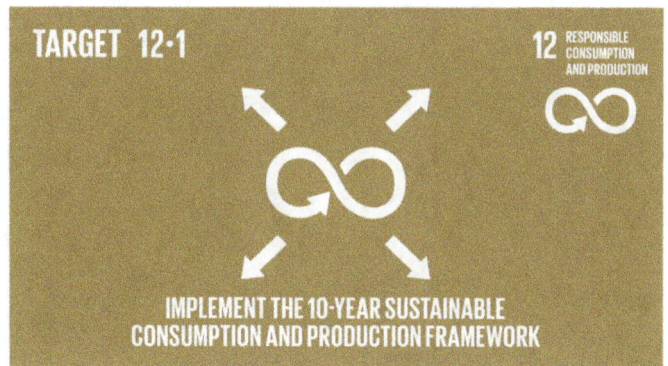

Implement the 10-Year Framework of Programmes on Sustainable Consumption and Production Patterns, all countries taking action, with developed countries taking the lead, taking into account the development and capabilities of developing countries

- Indicator 12.1.1: Number of countries developing, adopting or implementing policy instruments aimed at supporting the shift to sustainable consumption and production

The 10-Year Framework of Programmes on Sustainable Consumption was adopted at the UN Conference on Sustainable Development in Rio in 2012.

To reach Target 12.1, all government ministries and industrial sectors need to partake in stewardship of the one planet we have. There's a big global data gap for Indicator 12.1.1, although all countries who've reported as of 2023 have a sustainable consumption and production plan.[cxcvii]

Target 12.1 asks for the developed countries to take the lead, as they tend to have the worst outcomes in sustainable production and consumption. The US has such a plan, but Canada doesn't have data. Most EU countries have a plan, though there are some large exceptions without data. Japan, Israel, and New Zealand don't have data, but Australia has a plan.

Target 12.2

By 2030, achieve the sustainable management and efficient use of natural resources

- Indicator 12.2.1: Material footprint, material footprint per capita, and material footprint per GDP
- Indicator 12.2.2: Domestic material consumption, domestic material consumption per capita, and domestic material consumption per GDP

Domestic material consumption is all the materials used by an economy, starting with the extraction of natural resources, any manufacturing or industrial processes, and follows the path of the materials along onto trade, use, disposal, and any related emissions. Target 12.2 hasn't specified how we'll know whether we've achieved sustainable management and efficient use of natural resources by 2030.

As of 2022, the global material footprint per capita was 12 tonnes, unchanged since the adoption of the SDGs in 2015, and equal to a kilogram of material footprint per dollar of economic output.[cxcviii]

The worst performers for domestic material consumption per capita as of 2022 were Canada and Chile, which both consumed more than 50 tonnes of materials. Measuring the efficiency of material use per dollar created in the economy, the worst performers were Guinea, Lesotho, Mongolia and Chad, which all consumed more than 10kg of materials per dollar of GDP.

Target 12.3

**By 2030, halve per capita global food waste at the retail and consumer levels and reduce
food losses along production and supply chains, including post-harvest losses**

- Indicator 12.3.1: (a) Food loss index and (b) food waste index

The UN Environment Programme prepares the Food Waste Index, which accounts for food loss from the farm, through to retail, and onto consumers.

The global Food Loss Index in 2021 was 98.3, measuring the percentage of food lost compared to the baseline of 2015, suggesting there's not been a reduction in the SDG period - off-track for a halving of global food waste by 2030.[199]

Target 12.4

By 2020, achieve the environmentally sound management of chemicals and all wastes throughout their life cycle, in accordance with agreed international frameworks, and significantly reduce their release to air, water and soil in order to minimize their adverse impacts on human health and the environment

- Indicator 12.4.1: Number of parties to international multilateral environmental agreements on hazardous waste, and other chemicals that meet their commitments and obligations in transmitting information as required by each relevant agreement
- Indicator 12.4.2: (a) Hazardous waste generated per capita; and (b) proportion of hazardous waste treated, by type of treatment

The international environmental agreements used to measure Indicator 12.4.1 include the:

- Rotterdam Convention on the international trade of hazardous chemicals and pesticides. All countries have ratified, except a few (USA, Angola, Tajikistan).
- Montreal Protocol of 1987 on ozone-depleting substances
- Minamata Convention on Mercury. Named after the Japanese city, after mercury poisoning from this toxic metal, known as Minamata disease, was first found here.
- Stockholm Convention on persistent organic pollutants (POPs). All countries have ratified it except the USA, Israel, Malaysia, and Haiti.

- Basel Convention of 1989 on transboundary hazardous waste disposal. Only the USA and Haiti haven't ratified.

The above agreements oblige its parties to report to the respective treaty secretariats. As of 2020, all parties gave all required information for the Montreal Protocol, three-quarter for the Rotterdam Convention, half for the Stockholm Convention, and 60% for the Basel Convention.[200]

A lot of countries don't have data for hazardous waste per capita as of 2021, but among those who do, Kazakhstan produced the most (9,624kg per capita).[201]

Indicator 12.4.2 measures the proportion of hazardous waste treated by type, though only a handful of countries reported how many tonnes they'd recycled, incinerated, sent to landfill, or managed another way. We're unable to measure if there's been a reduction by 2020 in the release of chemicals and hazardous waste to the environment, or if its impacts were minimised.

Target 12.5

By 2030, substantially reduce waste generation through prevention, reduction, recycling and reuse

- Indicator 12.5.1: National recycling rate, tons of material recycled

In the waste hierarchy, if we've neither prevented, reduced, or reused waste, we at least need to ensure it's recycled, rather than going to landfill.

A lot of countries don't have data for the measure of municipal waste recycled within their borders, though the developed countries are the most pertinent, given they create the most waste. Among those with data, the largest amounts recycled as of 2022 were in the US (62 million tonnes) and Germany (35 million tonnes).[202] Since 2015, this amount has stayed the same in Germany, and there was a reduction of only about a million tonnes in the US.

Target 12.6

Encourage companies, especially large and transnational companies, to adopt sustainable practices and to integrate sustainability information into their reporting cycle

- Indicator 12.6.1: Number of companies publishing sustainability reports

The country with the most companies publishing sustainability reports as of 2022 was the US, leading with 1,293.[203]

Worldwide, a total of 5,203 companies produced sustainability reports in 2022, up from 2,276 in 2016.[204]

Target 12.7

Promote public procurement practices that are sustainable, in accordance with national policies and priorities

- Indicator 12.7.1: Number of countries implementing sustainable public procurement policies and action plans

High-income OECD countries spend an estimated 12% of GDP on public procurement and 30% in developing countries.[205] Given their purchasing power, it's important government purchases align with the SDGs, not only considering what's the best value for money when assessing tenders, but factoring in sustainability.

Few countries outside the OECD have data for this Indicator as of 2022.[206] The leader is the United States, which has a 'high' level of implementation of sustainable public procurement policies. Two high-income countries with low implementation of sustainable public procurement plans are Spain and Czechia.

Target 12.8

**By 2030, ensure that people everywhere have the relevant information and awareness for
sustainable development and lifestyles in harmony with nature**

- Indicator 12.8.1: Extent to which (i) global citizenship education and (ii) education for sustainable development are mainstreamed in (a) national education policies; (b) curricula; (c) teacher education; and (d) student assessment

Target 12.8 is the same as Target 4.7, relating to education on sustainable development and global citizenship. Indicator 12.8.1 is a duplicate of 4.7.1, and later to come, Indicator 13.3.1.

Target 12.A

**Support developing countries to strengthen their scientific and technological capacity to
move towards more sustainable patterns of consumption and production**

- Indicator 12.a.1: Installed renewable energy-generating capacity in developing and developed countries (in watts per capita)

The sole indicator of Target 12.a measures renewable energy capacity, in contrast to the other facets of sustainable production and consumption, and their scientific and technological underpinnings.

Bhutan is the developing country with the largest renewable energy capacity per capita as of 2022 (3,000 watts).[207]

Many developing countries still languish with less than 10 watts of renewables capacity per capita. Sub-Saharan Africa is the region with the lowest capacity, with 37 watts per capita, on par with the least developed countries, in contrast with the worldwide renewable capacity of 268 watts per capita.

Target 12.B

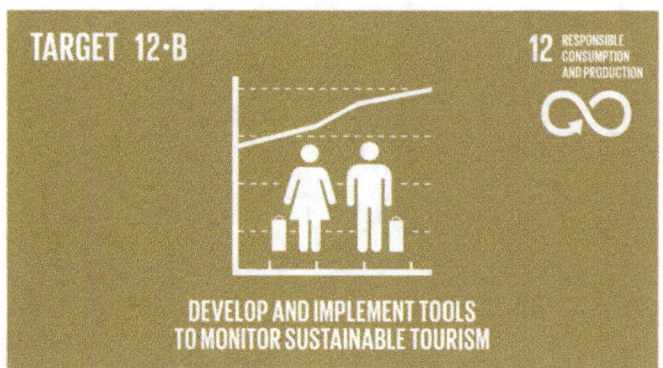

Develop and implement tools to monitor sustainable development impacts for sustainable tourism that creates jobs and promotes local culture and products

- Indicator 12.b.1: Implementation of standard accounting tools to monitor the economic and environmental aspects of tourism sustainability

Costa Rica and Mexico score the highest for implementation for Indicator 12.b.1, followed by Australia and the Philippines.[208]

Target 12.C

Rationalize inefficient fossil-fuel subsidies that encourage wasteful consumption by removing market distortions, in accordance with national circumstances, including by restructuring taxation and phasing out those harmful subsidies, where they exist, to reflect their environmental impacts, taking fully into account the specific needs and conditions of developing countries and minimizing the possible adverse impacts on their development in a manner that protects the poor and the affected communities

- Indicator 12.c.1: Amount of fossil-fuel subsidies (production and consumption) per unit of GDP

The countries with the biggest share of GDP going toward fossil fuel subsidies as of 2021 were Venezuela, Algeria, Libya, Iran, Turkmenistan and Uzbekistan.[209] Each of these countries had greater than 10% of their GDP spent on fossil fuel subsidies, the highest in Venezuela (21%). The proportion of gross world product spent on fossil fuel subsidies has risen and fallen since 2015 - its highest level in 2021 (0.85%), from a 2015 baseline of 0.71%. Qatar, Kuwait, UAE, Bahrain, Saudi Arabia, and Turkmenistan each spent more than $1,000 of subsidies per capita.[210] The highest was Qatar, with $2,535, close to a doubling since 2015.[211] Worldwide, there was a similar trajectory in the SDG period for spending per unit of GDP, with $92 spent per global citizen, up from $71 in 2015.[212] In total, the biggest spender was Iran, which spent $59 billion on fossil fuel subsidies, out of a global total of $731 billion for 2021.[213]

Goal #13

Take urgent action to combat climate change and its impacts

Target 13.1

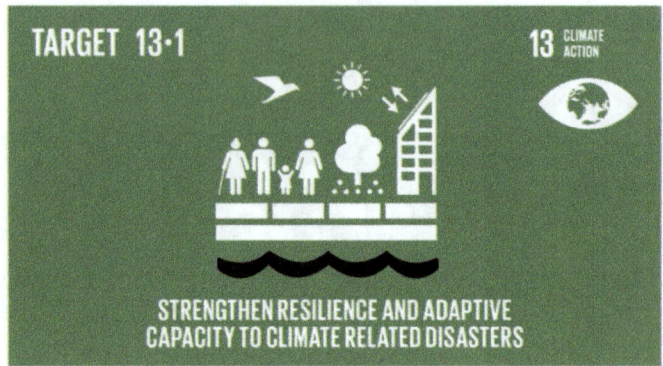

Strengthen resilience and adaptive capacity to climate-related hazards and natural disasters in all countries

- Indicator 13.1.1: Number of deaths, missing persons and directly affected persons attributed to disasters per 100,000 population
- Indicator 13.1.2: Number of countries that adopt and implement national disaster risk reduction strategies in line with the Sendai Framework for Disaster Risk Reduction 2015–2030
- Indicator 13.1.3: Proportion of local governments that adopt and implement local disaster risk reduction strategies in line with national disaster risk reduction strategies

With the mention of the Sendai Framework, we're reminded of this Target's similarities with Target's 1.5 and 11.b.

Indicator 13.1.1 matches Indicator 11.5.1, so we can refer to Target 11.5 for its progress. Indicator 13.1.2 is the same as Indicator 1.5.3, and Indicator 13.1.3 a duplicate of Indicator 11.b.2, making copies of all Target 13.1's official Indicators.

Target 13.2

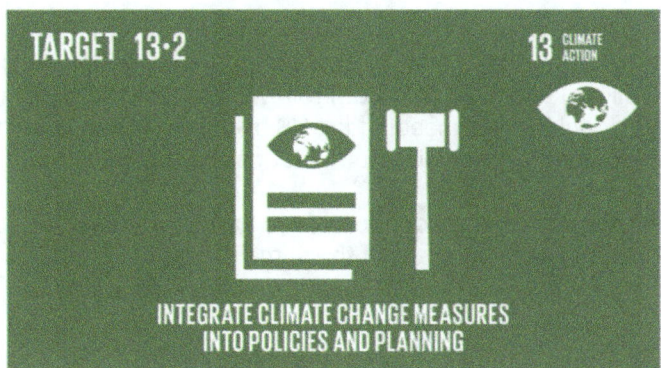

Integrate climate change measures into national policies, strategies and planning

- Indicator 13.2.1: Number of countries with nationally determined contributions, long-term strategies, national adaptation plans and adaptation communications, as reported to the secretariat of the United Nations Framework Convention on Climate Change
- Indicator 13.2.2: Total greenhouse gas emissions per year

The Paris Agreement is a treaty within the framework of the UN Framework Convention on Climate Change, the latter adopted in 1992. The UNFCCC has 198 signatories, of which 195 have ratified the Paris Agreement.

The UNFCCC Secretariat registers the 'nationally determined contributions' (NDCs) mentioned in Indicator 13.2.1, which are available online to check each country's progress. All parties to the Paris Agreement have provided a first NDC, and as of 2023, only 17 had supplied a second NDC.

The UNFCCC calls on parties to keep inventory of their domestic greenhouse gas emissions. Each greenhouse gas has a different potential for global warming. For example, nitrogen trifluoride has a global warming potential 17,200 times greater than carbon dioxide over the span of a century, but each greenhouse gas stays in the atmosphere for different lengths. The concentration of carbon dioxide humans have emitted to the atmosphere far exceeds other greenhouse gases, and stays in the atmosphere up to a millennium.

The country with the largest greenhouse gas emissions in 2023 was China, emitting the equivalent of 14 billion tonnes of carbon dioxide.[214] The US (6 billion) and India (4 billion) followed, bearing in mind India and China have populations exceeding the US by a billion each, and the US bears the greatest responsibility for historical emissions.

Since 2015, the year of the adoption of the Paris Agreement, annual global emissions have been about the same through to 2023 (53 billion tonnes).[215]

Greenhouse gas emissions, 2023

Greenhouse gas emissions¹ include carbon dioxide, methane and nitrous oxide from all sources, including land-use change. They are measured in tonnes of carbon dioxide-equivalents² over a 100-year timescale.

Scale: No data | 0 t | 10 million t | 30 million t | 100 million t | 300 million t | 1 billion t | 3 billion t | 10 billion t

Data source: Jones et al. (2024)
Note: Land-use change emissions can be negative.
OurWorldinData.org/co2-and-greenhouse-gas-emissions | CC BY

Target 13.3

**Improve education, awareness-raising and human and institutional capacity on climate
change mitigation, adaptation, impact reduction and early warning**

- Indicator 13.3.1: Extent to which (i) global citizenship education and (ii) education for sustainable development are mainstreamed in (a) national education policies; (b) curricula; (c) teacher education; and (d) student assessment

Indicator 13.3.1 duplicates Indicators 4.7.1 and 12.8.1, except Target 13.3 focuses on raising awareness of climate change, in contrast to education for sustainable development as a whole.

Target 13.A

Implement the commitment undertaken by developed-country parties to the United Nations Framework Convention on Climate Change to a goal of mobilizing jointly $100 billion annually by 2020 from all sources to address the needs of developing countries in the context of meaningful mitigation actions and transparency on implementation and fully operationalize the Green Climate Fund through its capitalization as soon as possible

- Indicator 13.a.1: Amounts provided and mobilized in United States dollars per year in relation to the continued existing collective mobilization goal of the $100 billion commitment through to 2025

The text of Target 13.a specifies a 2020 aim, but developed countries missed this, unable to provide the committed $100 billion to the Green Climate Fund for the developing world. The official Indicator for this Target now has an extension to 2025.

In the years between 2015 and 2020, the world paid only a total of around $50 billion per year to the Green Climate Fund, half the modest commitment of $100 billion, equal to 0.1% of gross world product (GWP), an annual figure which rose only $5 billion since 2015.[216]

Target 13.B

Promote mechanisms for raising capacity for effective climate change-related planning and management in least developed countries and small island developing States, including focusing on women, youth and local and marginalized communities

- Indicator 13.b.1: Number of least developed countries and small island developing States with nationally determined contributions, long-term strategies, national adaptation plans and adaptation communications, as reported to the secretariat of the United Nations Framework Convention on Climate Change

As we saw in Target 13.2, all countries have provided a NDC.

As of 2023, of the 45 least developed countries, 19 have provided national adaptation plans, as had 11 of the 39 Small Island Developing States.[217] It's crucial for both these groups to plan for climate change adaptation, as it's likely to affect the vulnerable the most.

Goal #14

Conserve and sustainably use the oceans, seas and marine resources for sustainable development

Target 14.1

By 2025, prevent and significantly reduce marine pollution of all kinds, in particular from land-based activities, including marine debris and nutrient pollution

- Indicator 14.1.1: (a) Index of coastal eutrophication; and (b) plastic debris density

Eutrophication occurs due to excess nutrients in a water body, such as nitrogen and phosphorus.

To measure this, as the first part of Indicator 14.1.1, we can measure the levels of a type of chlorophyll, the key to photosynthesis in green plants and algae. The concentration of chlorophyll acts as a proxy for eutrophication, as excessive nutrients in a water body can result in algal blooms, sucking out oxygen from the water, depriving other lifeforms which call it home. The measure is how much chlorophyll on each country's coast varies from the global average, with the highest 2022 levels in Trinidad & Tobago (20%).[218]

As of 2023, the world's laggards in beach litter were Egypt, Nepal, Cyprus, and Gambia - each with greater than 10 million items of plastic per square kilometre on their shores - although more than a dozen countries with coasts didn't have 2023 data for this measure.[219] The 2022 global average was 224,000 pieces of litter per square kilometre of beach, a reduction from the baseline at the start of the SDG period of 31 million pieces of litter per km^2, following a rise in 2018 up to 35 million.

Target 14.2

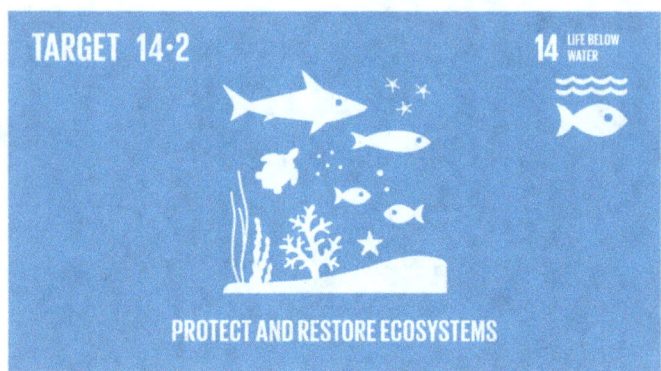

By 2020, sustainably manage and protect marine and coastal ecosystems to avoid significant adverse impacts, including by strengthening their resilience, and take action for their restoration in order to achieve healthy and productive oceans

- Indicator 14.2.1: Number of countries using ecosystem-based approaches to managing marine areas

Progress for Indicator 14.2.1, measuring countries' plans to manage the environment of their coastal zones, is sparing as of 2023, so we're unable to measure whether Target 14.2 was met by 2020.

Target 14.3

Minimize and address the impacts of ocean acidification, including through enhanced scientific cooperation at all levels

- Indicator 14.3.1: Average marine acidity (pH) measured at agreed suite of representative sampling stations

In the climate system, the hydrosphere of the Earth's water, and the atmosphere of gases held in place by gravity, are key components. Absorption of carbon dioxide by the oceans can ease some of the effects of climate change, but only up to a point, before it begins to affect its chemical balance, impacting life within.

We can view the levels of ocean acidification through resources such as GOA-ON, which allows us to see how ocean ecosystems respond to elevated levels of acidification, and SOCAT (Surface Ocean CO^2 Atlas), which measures the degree to which the ocean absorbs CO^2.

The work of Indicator 14.3.1 is the responsibility of the International Oceanographic Commission, a sub-body within UNESCO. This Target and Indicator asks what the average acidity or alkalinity of the ocean is - in large part, caused by the absorption of carbon dioxide from the atmosphere. Using a sampling station in Hawaii, the annual average pH as of September 2022 was 8.05, down 0.2 since the adoption of the SDGs in 2015.[220] The lower the pH, the more acidic, with the threshold from neutral to acidic being a pH below 7 - the current pH of 8.07 demonstrating moderate alkalinity.

Target 14.4

By 2020, effectively regulate harvesting and end overfishing, illegal, unreported and unregulated fishing and destructive fishing practices and implement science-based management plans, in order to restore fish stocks in the shortest time feasible, at least to levels that can produce maximum sustainable yield as determined by their biological characteristics

- Indicator 14.4.1: Proportion of fish stocks within biologically sustainable levels

Target 14.4 looks at fishing practices destroying the health of aquatic ecosystems, including those which are illegal, unreported, and unregulated.

As of 2021, too many countries are without data to see if the 2020 aim of Target 14.4 was met.[221] Among those who've reported, countries which had no sustainable fish stocks were Lebanon, Pakistan, Poland, Costa Rica, El Salvador and Egypt.

Of the top 10 countries with the biggest fishing industries, China, India, Vietnam, and Russia haven't reported data for Indicator 14.4.1. Worldwide, as of 2021, 62% of fish stocks were sustainable, and the rest overexploited - unchanged since 2015.[222]

Target 14.5

By 2020, conserve at least 10 per cent of coastal and marine areas, consistent with national and international law and based on the best available scientific information

- Indicator 14.5.1: Coverage of protected areas in relation to marine areas

Among protected areas, there are six categories of protection: the top tier being 'strict nature reserves' and 'wilderness areas,' and the bottom tier, 'protected areas,' which permit the use of natural resources in a sustainable manner. The World Database on Protected Areas by Protected Planet collates all these protected areas, including other effective area-based conservation measures. Key biodiversity areas are ecosystems which meet a criteria critical to prevent extinctions, and protected areas are at the forefront of conserving such environments. The key international treaty relating to biodiversity is the Convention on Biological Diversity (CBD). A set of targets within the framework of the CBD, known as the Aichi Targets, named after the Japanese prefecture of their adoption, was set for the decade 2010-2020. Target 14.5 of the SDGs draws from Aichi Target #11, the aim of which was to protect 10% of marine areas, which the world met, with 13% protected by 2020.[223] Among the world leaders were Palau and Monaco (100%), and France and Kazakhstan (50%), the latter in the case of the inland Caspian Sea. The global percentage of protected marine key biodiversity areas as of 2023 was 45%, not much improved since 2015.[224]

Target 14.6

By 2020, prohibit certain forms of fisheries subsidies which contribute to overcapacity and overfishing, eliminate subsidies that contribute to illegal, unreported and unregulated fishing and refrain from introducing new such subsidies, recognizing that appropriate and effective special and differential treatment for developing and least developed countries should be an integral part of the World Trade Organization fisheries subsidies negotiation

- Indicator 14.6.1: Degree of implementation of international instruments aiming to combat illegal, unreported and unregulated fishing

The primary treaty governing international fisheries and maritime matters is the 1982 UN Convention on the Law of the Sea, supplemented by the UN Fish Stocks Agreement, focused on fisheries management. The UN's Food and Agriculture Organisation oversees several other agreements, including guidelines by which the flag state, under which a vessel sails, bears some responsibility - as well as a code of conduct for responsible fisheries. International agreements exist to enforce illegal catches at ports, and countries which are party to these agreements are obliged to inspect vessels in their waters, to counter illegal evasion. For the measure of implementation of these treaties, 5 is the highest score, and 1 the lowest. The world scored 4 as of 2024, up from 3 in 2018.[225] Countries with scores of 1 as of 2024 include Azerbaijan, Congo, Kuwait, and Dominican Republic, though many countries don't have data for this measure.

Target 14.7

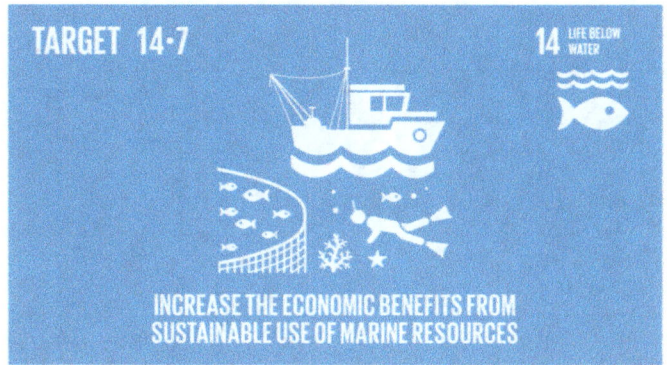

By 2030, increase the economic benefits to small island developing States and least developed countries from the sustainable use of marine resources, including through sustainable management of fisheries, aquaculture and tourism

- Indicator 14.7.1: Sustainable fisheries as a proportion of GDP in small island developing States, least developed countries and all countries

Sustainable fishery stocks have declined from 90% in the mid-70s, to only 67% at the adoption of the SDGs.[226] The impact of this on the livelihoods of fishing communities in the most vulnerable countries can be acute, so yields need to be sustainable to help fishing communities over the long-term.

A reflection of how dependent a country is on fishing is the percentage of its GDP occupied by fisheries. Sierra Leone and Gambia had the highest reliance on sustainable fisheries as of 2021.[227] 0.81% of the GDP of least developed countries came from sustainable fisheries, a decrease from 1.25% in 2015 - off-track to increase the economic benefits from sustainable use of marine resources by 2030. For the Small Island Developing States, it was 0.51%, unchanged since 2015.

Target 14.A

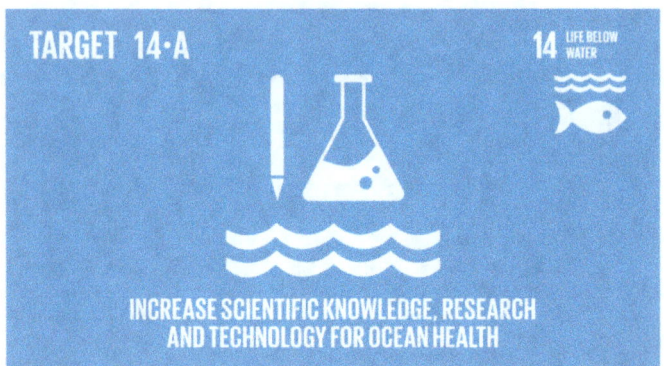

Increase scientific knowledge, develop research capacity and transfer marine technology, taking into account the Intergovernmental Oceanographic Commission Criteria and Guidelines on the Transfer of Marine Technology, in order to improve ocean health and to enhance the contribution of marine biodiversity to the development of developing countries, in particular small island developing States and least developed countries

- Indicator 14.a.1: Proportion of total research budget allocated to research in the field of marine technology

Part XIV of the UN Convention on the Law of the Sea enjoins states to cooperate on the development and transfer of:

"...marine science and marine technology on fair and reasonable terms and conditions."

The Intergovernmental Oceanographic Commission Criteria and Guidelines mentioned in the text of Target 14.a guide how to put the above into effect.

As of 2022, the leaders in funding of ocean science and research were Norway and Peru, each spending greater than 5% of GDP on such efforts, compared to worldwide expenditure equivalent to 1.1% of gross world product, down from 1.5% in 2015.[228]

Target 14.B

Provide access for small-scale artisanal fishers to marine resources and markets

- Indicator 14.b.1: Degree of application of a legal/regulatory/policy/institutional framework which recognizes and protects access rights for small-scale fisheries

The FAO issues Voluntary Guidelines for Securing Sustainable Small-Scale Fisheries, the purposes of which are to improve food security and reduce poverty.

The measure for protections of small-scale fisheries along such guidelines is a 1-5 scale, 5 being the highest and 1 the lowest. As of 2024, the countries with the lowest score among those with data are:

- Burundi and Nepal (both landlocked)
- Dominican Republic
- Libya
- Bosnia and Herzegovina (which has a 20-kilometre coastline)[229]

The global score for this measure was 4.

Target 14.C

Enhance the conservation and sustainable use of oceans and their resources by implementing international law as reflected in the United Nations Convention on the Law of the Sea, which provides the legal framework for the conservation and sustainable use of oceans and their resources, as recalled in paragraph 158 of "The future we want"

- Indicator 14.c.1: Number of countries making progress in ratifying, accepting and implementing through legal, policy and institutional frameworks, ocean-related instruments that implement international law, as reflected in the United Nations Convention on the Law of the Sea, for the conservation and sustainable use of the oceans and their resources

Target 14.c is asking whether countries have acceded to the Law of the Sea, and the extent to which they've implemented it.

Countries which aren't parties to the treaty include the USA, Peru, Venezuela, Eritrea, Türkiye, Syria and Israel. Several Central Asian countries which only have shores on the inland Caspian Sea aren't parties, and landlocked South Sudan isn't either. Beyond this, a dozen other countries have signed the convention, but not ratified it.

The least progress in implementing the convention has been in Iraq and landlocked Burundi, though not all parties have data for implementation of the Law of the Sea as of 2023.

Goal #15

Protect, restore and promote sustainable use of terrestrial ecosystems, sustainably manage forests, combat desertification, and halt and reverse land degradation and halt biodiversity loss

Target 15.1

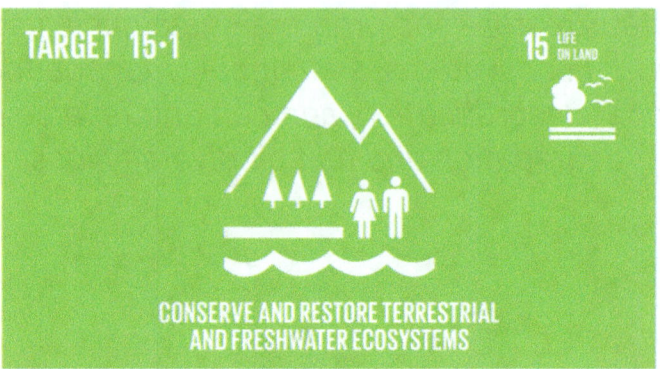

By 2020, ensure the conservation, restoration and sustainable use of terrestrial and inland freshwater ecosystems and their services, in particular forests, wetlands, mountains and drylands, in line with obligations under international agreements

- Indicator 15.1.1: Forest area as a proportion of total land area
- Indicator 15.1.2: Proportion of important sites for terrestrial and freshwater biodiversity that are covered by protected areas, by ecosystem type

Target 15.1 is the sister goal of Target 14.2, in this instance, focused on terrestrial and freshwater biodiversity. According to the World Database on Protected Areas, as of 2024, there are 293,704 protected areas, both on land and at sea.[230]

This Target's aim is for 2020, in line with the Aichi Biodiversity Targets and Strategic Plan for Biodiversity 2011-2020, both part of the Convention on Biological Diversity. The Kunming-Montreal Global Biodiversity Framework has now succeeded the Strategic Plan, providing new biodiversity goals and targets through to the end of the SDG period and beyond to mid-century.

The countries with greater than 90% forest as a proportion of all land are Gabon, Equatorial Guinea, the Guianas, the Solomon Islands and Palau.[231]

The region with the least is the drylands band across the Sahara and Horn of Africa, through to the Middle East and Central Asia. The global share of forest cover on land in 2020 was 31%, unchanged since the adoption of the Goals in 2015 - conserving forest cover but not restoring.[232]

The archipelago of the Seychelles has the highest proportion of protected land as of 2022, with 61%, followed by Venezuela.[233] As of 2021, 15% of Earth's land was a protected area.[234] Around a dozen European countries protect the highest percentage of land and freshwater. Other leaders as of 2023 were Namibia, Zimbabwe, Equatorial Guinea, and the Guianas.[235] Worldwide, this share was 44% in 2023 for both freshwater and terrestrial key biodiversity areas, little changed since 2015.[236]

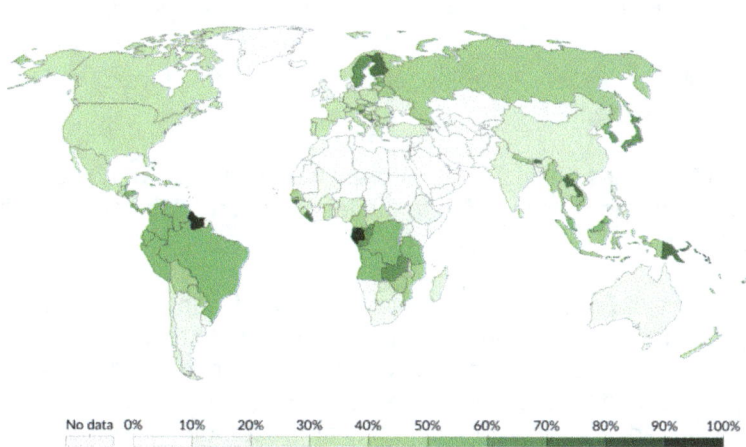

Target 15.2

By 2020, promote the implementation of sustainable management of all types of forests, halt deforestation, restore degraded forests and substantially increase afforestation and reforestation globally

- Indicator 15.2.1: Progress towards sustainable forest management

Target 15.2 focuses on sustainable forest management, which some readers may be familiar with due to the logos of certifying bodies such as the FSC and PEFC.

Côte d'Ivoire and Egypt took the biggest backward step in sustainable forest management by deforestation as of 2020, both reversing 3% of forest cover.[237] In the same year, global forest cover stayed about the same, suggesting the 2020 aim to halt deforestation was met, without restoring degraded forests, or increasing afforestation and reforestation.

Across the planet, the region with the greatest concentration of biomass is in the Guianas, with greater than 300 tonnes per hectare.[238] By contrast, worldwide average biomass was 118 tonnes per hectare of land above the surface.

Venezuela, Senegal, and Uzbekistan have the highest percentage of protected forests (>90%), whereas the countries in the boreal latitudes of Canada, Scandinavia and Russia protect less than 10%.[239] Several other countries with high forest cover have low protections, including Guyana.

The worldwide share was 17% as of 2020, unchanged since the start of the SDG period in 2015.

58% of global forest was under a long-term forest management plan as of 2020, a couple percentage increase from 2015.[240]

Canada has by far the most hectares of forest certified by the FSC or PEFC for sustainable use (156 million hectares).[241] The global total of certified forest was 444 million hectares as of 2023, up from 397 million in 2015.

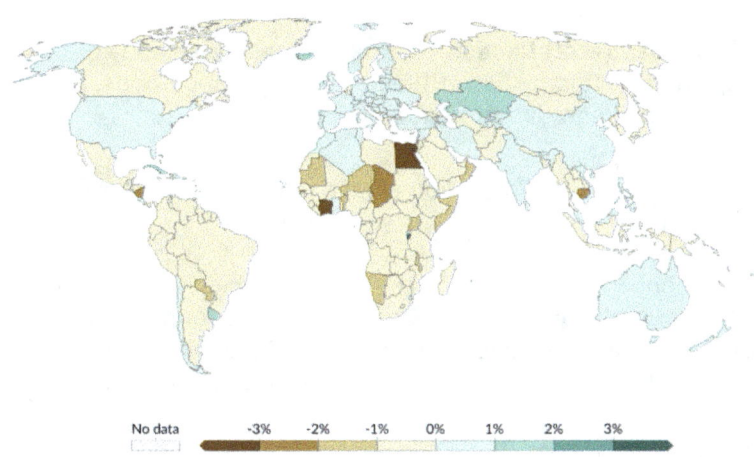

Annual change in forest area, 2020
The annual net change in forested area as a percentage of total forest area. Negative values indicate a net loss of forest, and positive values indicate a net gain.

Data source: Food and Agriculture Organization of the United Nations
OurWorldInData.org/forests-and-deforestation | CC BY

Target 15.3

By 2030, combat desertification, restore degraded land and soil, including land affected by desertification, drought and floods, and strive to achieve a land degradation-neutral world

- Indicator 15.3.1: Proportion of land that is degraded over total land area

We want to conserve and protect nature, part of which involves ensuring we don't degrade the quality of the soil, which is the foundation for so much of life, as climate change worsens desertification. Mitigating and preventing land degradation allows ecosystems to function and assures food security.

As of 2019, the country with the highest proportion of degraded land, by a large margin, is Mexico (71%), with worldwide degradation standing at 15%, with only one year of global data, so we're unable to gauge if there's been a restoration or halting of degraded land.[242]

Target 15.4

By 2030, ensure the conservation of mountain ecosystems, including their biodiversity, in order to enhance their capacity to provide benefits that are essential for sustainable development

- Indicator 15.4.1: Coverage by protected areas of important sites for mountain biodiversity
- Indicator 15.4.2: (a) Mountain Green Cover Index and (b) proportion of degraded mountain land

The Mountain Green Cover Index measures changes in vegetation in mountain regions, which many have high proportions of, exceeding 90%. Several countries of the Sahara and Sahel have the least vegetation on their mountains. Worldwide, the Mountain Green Cover Index stands at 78%. As of 2018, the countries with the largest share of degraded mountain land were Portugal, Tunisia, Eswatini, and Vietnam, all with greater than 4% degradation. The worldwide proportion was less than 2%, a fractional increase since 2015.

Global coverage of protected areas in mountains of key biodiversity areas was 40% as of 2022, a minor increase from 38% from 2015, suggesting the conservation aspect of Target 15.4 was on track for 2030.

Target 15.5

Take urgent and significant action to reduce the degradation of natural habitats, halt the loss of biodiversity and, by 2020, protect and prevent the extinction of threatened species

- Indicator 15.5.1: Red List Index

The Red List Index tracks trends for the extinction risk of each species, and progress on biodiversity targets, and is part of the IUCN Red List of Threatened Species, established by the IUCN (International Union for Conservation of Nature).

Too many species face the threat of extinction amid a startling rate of decline from a plethora of causes, including invasive alien species, climate change, or destruction at the hands of human drivers.

The Red List considers in its criteria whether:

- a species faces endangerment in its existing population
- the speed at which the species' population is declining
- how distributed the species' existing population is

The categories of highest risk of extinction in the wild are:

- Vulnerable
- Endangered
- Critically Endangered

At the other end of the conservation spectrum are those species the IUCN considers 'Least Concern,' for which the health of their populations, ecosystems, and habitats are secure for now.

The Red List Index is a measure from 0 to 1, 0 suggesting all species are extinct. Measured across countries, the lowest Red List Index figure by a wide margin is in Mauritius, home of the extinct dodo, scoring 0.38 as of 2024, followed by Sri Lanka with 0.55.[243] The worldwide 2024 Red List Index score is 0.72 - unchanged since 2015. Target 15.5's aim to protect and prevent the extinction of threatened species by 2020, and to halt the loss of biodiversity, has failed.

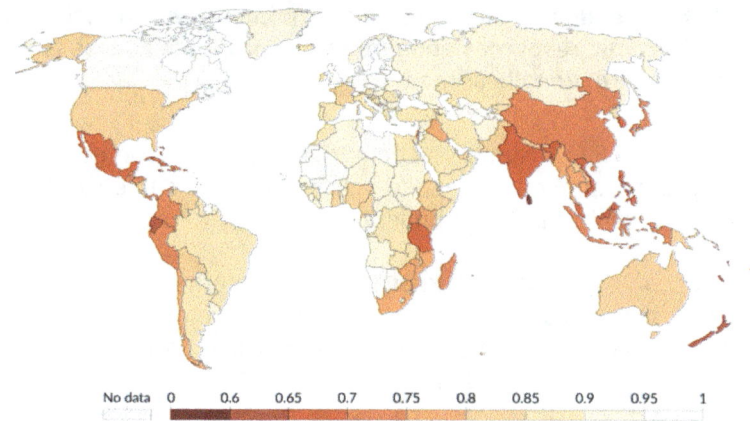

Target 15.6

Promote fair and equitable sharing of the benefits arising from the utilization of genetic resources and promote appropriate access to such resources, as internationally agreed

- Indicator 15.6.1: Number of countries that have adopted legislative, administrative and policy frameworks to ensure fair and equitable sharing of benefits

The key treaty of relevance for Target 15.6 is the International Treaty on Plant Genetic Resources for Food and Agriculture, explored within Target 2.5. The intention for Contracting Party countries is to provide access to, and transfer of, knowledge and materials.

The Contracting Parties use a reporting platform called the Access and Benefit Sharing Clearing House, established by the Nagoya Protocol on Access and Benefit-sharing. The Nagoya Protocol is an addition to the Convention on Biological Diversity, named after the Japanese city of its adoption by the Convention's parties, and aims for fair access to genetic resources.

There's little uniformity among the Contracting Parties on who's adopted relevant legislation. Only 137 of the 192 UN Member States have ratified the Nagoya Protocol, and 152 are parties to the International Treaty on Plant Genetic Resources for Food and Agriculture.

Target 15.7

Take urgent action to end poaching and trafficking of protected species of flora and fauna and address both demand and supply of illegal wildlife products

- Indicator 15.7.1: Proportion of traded wildlife that was poached or illicitly trafficked

The key treaty relevant to Target 15.7 is the CITES (Convention on International Trade in Endangered Species of Wild Fauna and Flora).

The Checklist of CITES Species lists species, and the degree to which each is protected in trade. Parties to CITES are required to report annual illegal trade reports of wildlife seizures, information which is stored in the CITES Illegal Trade Database.

The UN Office on Drugs and Crime has issued the most recent World Wildlife Crime Report in 2024, which reported illegal trade in 162 countries across 4,000 plant and animal species for the 2015-2021 period - 3,250 species of which are protected under CITES.

Target 15.8

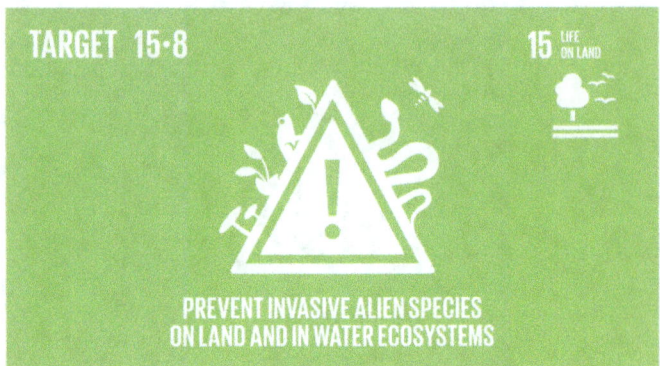

By 2020, introduce measures to prevent the introduction and significantly reduce the impact of invasive alien species on land and water ecosystems and control or eradicate the priority species

- Indicator 15.8.1: Proportion of countries adopting relevant national legislation and adequately resourcing the prevention or control of invasive alien species

From 2010 to 2020, Aichi Biodiversity Target #9 guided all countries which were party to the Convention on Biological Diversity, in relation to the control, eradication, and prevention of introduction of invasive alien species.

Article 6 of the Convention on Biological Diversity requires each party to develop a national biodiversity strategy and action plan (NBSAP). By comparing this to Aichi Target #9, we can get a sense of a country's progress toward Indicator 15.8.1. Alignment of NBSAP's to Aichi Target #9 was widespread across parties to the CBD as of 2020, with a dozen or so exceptions, including the US, which isn't a party.

We can measure whether a country is providing ample resources for the prevention or control of invasive alien species by budgeting for it. On this measure, there's not much of a pattern on which countries introduced appropriate measures as of 2020, the end date for Target 15.8.

Target 15.9

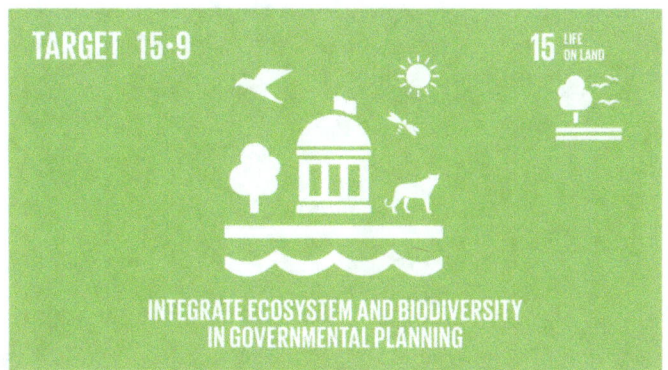

By 2020, integrate ecosystem and biodiversity values into national and local planning, development processes, poverty reduction strategies and accounts

- Indicator 15.9.1: (a) Number of countries that have established national Targets in accordance with or similar to Aichi Biodiversity Target 2 of the Strategic Plan for Biodiversity 2011–2020 in their national biodiversity strategy and action plans and the progress reported towards these Targets; and (b) integration of biodiversity into national accounting and reporting systems, defined as implementation of the System of Environmental-Economic Accounting

Target 15.1 already mentioned the CBD's Strategic Plan for Biodiversity 2011-2020. The System of Environmental-Economic Accounting is a framework used by the UN, allowing us to observe the impact on the economy from the environment and vice versa.

The requisite planning, as called for by Target 15.9 upon countries, relates to the NSBAPs referred to in the previous Target.

For national adoption of the System of Environmental-Economic Accounting, there's a split across the globe as of 2023, with little uniformity or pattern between those who've implemented the framework, although there's no earlier data to see if the 2020 aim of Target 15.9 was met.[244]

Target 15.A

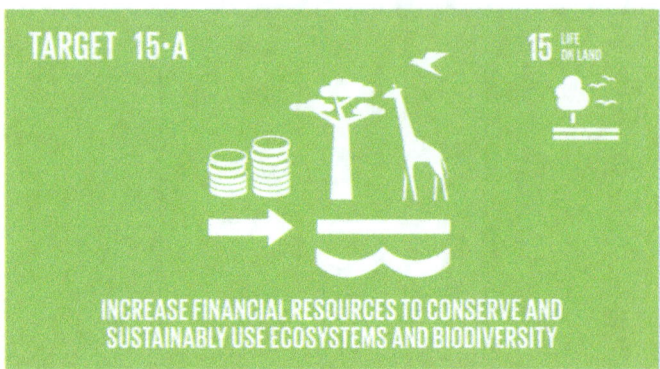

Mobilize and significantly increase financial resources from all sources to conserve and sustainably use biodiversity and ecosystems

- Indicator 15.a.1: (a) Official development assistance on conservation and sustainable use of biodiversity; and (b) revenue generated and finance mobilized from biodiversity-relevant economic instruments

Target 15.a measures what level of aid from high-income donor countries goes toward biodiversity. India was the biggest recipient in 2022, receiving $626 million.[245] The largest 2022 donors for foreign aid earmarked for biodiversity were France and Germany, who each donated over $2 billion. For most developing regions, in the SDG period, aid for biodiversity has gone up and done, though by 2021, the most recent year of data, was back to the same level as 2015.

Target 15.B

Mobilize significant resources from all sources and at all levels to finance sustainable forest management and provide adequate incentives to developing countries to advance such management, including for conservation and reforestation

- Indicator 15.b.1: (a) Official development assistance on conservation and sustainable use of biodiversity; and (b) revenue generated and finance mobilized from biodiversity-relevant economic instruments

Target 15.b is the same as the previous Target, with Indicators across both Targets the same, differing in their focus on sustainable forest management, in contrast to biodiversity.

Target 15.C

Enhance global support for efforts to combat poaching and trafficking of protected species, including by increasing the capacity of local communities to pursue sustainable livelihood opportunities

- Indicator 15.c.1: Proportion of traded wildlife that was poached or illicitly trafficked

Target 15.c recalls Target #15.7, with the same Indicator, focused on the illegal wildlife trade. Again, the centrality of the CITES treaty governs the actions of countries in relation to such practices.

Goal #16

Promote peaceful and inclusive societies for sustainable development, provide access to justice for all and build effective, accountable and inclusive institutions at all levels

Target 16.1

Significantly reduce all forms of violence and related death rates everywhere

- Indicator 16.1.1: Number of victims of intentional homicide per 100,000 population, by sex and age
- Indicator 16.1.2: Conflict-related deaths per 100,000 population, by sex, age and cause
- Indicator 16.1.3: Proportion of population subjected to (a) physical violence, (b) psychological violence and/or (c) sexual violence in the previous 12 months
- Indicator 16.1.4: Proportion of population that feel safe walking alone around the area they live after dark

Among countries with data, the highest homicide rate is in Jamaica, with 53 per 100,000 population in 2022.[246] By comparison, the worldwide homicide rate was 5 per 100,000, which showed no reduction since 2015.[247]

The highest number of conflict-related deaths in 2023 was in Ukraine (70,000), followed by Palestine (22,000) and Mexico (13,000), with only country-level data to observe reductions since 2015.[248]

Few countries have data for the Indicators relating to exposure to different forms of violence, and of feeling safe walking alone at night.

Target 16.2

End abuse, exploitation, trafficking and all forms of violence against and torture of children

- Indicator 16.2.1: Proportion of children aged 1–17 years who experienced any physical punishment and/or psychological aggression by caregivers in the past month
- Indicator 16.2.2: Number of victims of human trafficking per 100,000 population, by sex, age and form of exploitation
- Indicator 16.2.3: Proportion of young women and men aged 18–29 years who experienced sexual violence by age 18

All countries have ratified the UN Convention on Transnational Crime except Iran, Somalia, Papua New Guinea, Republic of Congo, South Sudan, and two Pacific nations. One of the protocols to this convention relates to human trafficking, focused on children and women. In 2010, the UN also adopted the UN Global Plan of Action to Combat Trafficking in Persons. There are plentiful regional initiatives of countries collaborating to combat trafficking, supplementing national efforts, as well as those under the auspices of the UN Office on Drugs and Crime.

In 2023, 78% of children experienced physical punishment and/or psychological aggression worldwide, very far from the aim to end all forms of violence against children.[249]

The highest number of human trafficking victims in 2022 were in India and Pakistan, each detecting around 2,000, though many countries which could be at risk are missing data for this Indicator.[250]

Indicator 16.2.2 disaggregates by sex and age. The biggest disparities in sex among countries with data in 2022 was in the UK, where trafficking of girls was more than tenfold, whereas in Tanzania, five times as many boys were trafficked.[251] For victims over 18, Belgium, Brazil, and Egypt had more than 10 times as many women trafficked as men.[252]

Many countries are missing data for the proportion of young women who experienced sexual violence before age 18. The highest reported rates were in the Democratic Republic of Congo, Mexico, and Trinidad & Tobago, each higher than 1 in 10, compared to a worldwide figure of 3%.[253] Few countries reported data for men who experienced sexual violence before age 18.

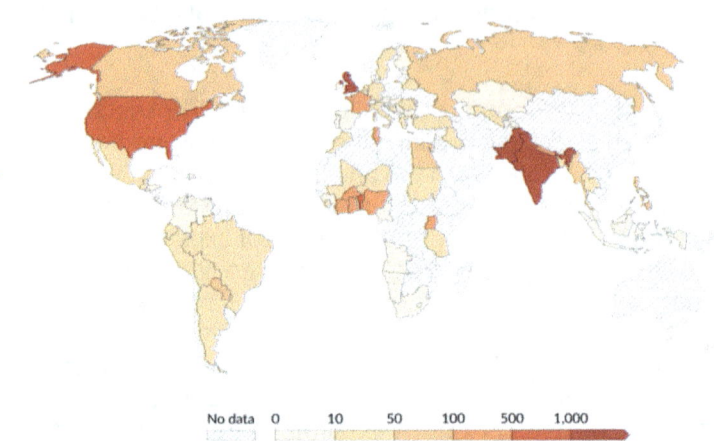

Human trafficking victims, 2022
The total number of human trafficking victims officially detected by national authorities.

Data source: UN Office on Drugs and Crime
Note: Trends should be interpreted with caution as data only includes detected victims, whose number also depends on legislative criteria and law enforcement practices.

Target 16.3

Promote the rule of law at the national and international levels and ensure equal access to justice for all

- Indicator 16.3.1: Proportion of victims of (a) physical, (b) psychological and/or (c) sexual violence in the previous 12 months who reported their victimization to competent authorities or other officially recognized conflict resolution mechanisms
- Indicator 16.3.2: Unsentenced detainees as a proportion of overall prison population
- Indicator 16.3.3: Proportion of the population who have experienced a dispute in the past two years and who accessed a formal or informal dispute resolution mechanism, by type of mechanism

An insufficient number of countries have supplied data to offer a global snapshot for the first and third Indicators of this Target as of 2022.

There are some notable absences from countries reporting data on the second Indicator, but for those which have reported, the highest rates as of 2021 were in Gabon and Bangladesh, where 80% of the prison populations were unsentenced.[254]

Target 16.4

By 2030, significantly reduce illicit financial and arms flows, strengthen the recovery and return of stolen assets and combat all forms of organized crime

- Indicator 16.4.1: Total value of inward and outward illicit financial flows (in current United States dollars)
- Indicator 16.4.2: Proportion of seized, found or surrendered arms whose illicit origin or context has been traced or established by a competent authority in line with international instruments

Illicit financial flows are money movements fitting into a variety of categories of criminality.

Of relevance to Indicator 16.4.1 is the UN Convention Against Corruption, which all member states of the UN are party to, except Eritrea and North Korea, and which Syria has signed, but not ratified.

For Indicator 16.4.2, one of the relevant UN bodies is the UN Office for Disarmament Affairs, as is Interpol (International Criminal Police Organization), which isn't part of the UN System.

There's an unfortunate great dearth of data for this Target's Indicators to see if the world is on track for a reduction by 2030 of illegal arms and finance, with only a handful of countries reporting.

Target 16.5

Substantially reduce corruption and bribery in all their forms

- Indicator 16.5.1: Proportion of persons who had at least one contact with a public official and who paid a bribe to a public official, or were asked for a bribe by those public officials, during the previous 12 months
- Indicator 16.5.2: Proportion of businesses that had at least one contact with a public official and that paid a bribe to a public official, or were asked for a bribe by those public officials during the previous 12 months

Many countries across the Middle East and North Africa don't have data for Indicator 16.5.1, nor China. Among other countries who do as of 2022, the highest prevalence of reported bribery was in the Democratic Republic of Congo, where 80% of Congolese reported paying a bribe, or had been asked to, by a public official.[255] Only country-level data is available to observe if there's been a substantial reduction in corruption.

Much less countries have reported data for bribery experienced by businesses at the hands of the government, but among those who have, Iraq had the highest prevalence in 2022 (50%), with a worldwide estimate of 15%.[256]

Target 16.6

Develop effective, accountable and transparent institutions at all levels

- Indicator 16.6.1: Primary government expenditures as a proportion of original approved budget, by sector (or by budget codes or similar)
- Indicator 16.6.2: Proportion of population satisfied with their last experience of public services

Indicator 16.6.1 considers the degree to which the approved budget of a country has kept within the budgeted amount.

Only about a dozen countries went over budget in 2023, and a similar number under.[257]

For Indicator 16.6.2, a half-dozen countries have provided data on satisfaction with public services as of 2021.[258]

Target 16.7

Ensure responsive, inclusive, participatory and representative decision-making at all levels

- Indicator 16.7.1: Proportions of positions in national and local institutions, including (a) the legislatures; (b) the public service; and (c) the judiciary, compared to national distributions, by sex, age, persons with disabilities and population groups
- Indicator 16.7.2: Proportion of population who believe decision-making is inclusive and responsive, by sex, age, disability and population group

The UN Security Council has passed resolutions relating to the inclusion of young people and women in decision-making. For women, this is due to the role they play in conflict prevention. Empowerment of youth offers stability. But without inclusion in decision-making, young men can be vulnerable to radicalisation.

Citizens need to feel as though their governments are open, and there's an opportunity to engage, and see their political views reflected. They need to be able to scrutinise government performance, and its individual members, which affects whether citizens feel they ought to carry out their own civic responsibility.

As of 2023, countries with the highest percentage of women in unicameral or lower houses of parliaments were Nicaragua, Cuba and Rwanda.[259] Each had proportions greater than half, and Mexico and UAE had gender parity. Since the adoption of the SDGs in 2015, the global share has risen from 21% to 26% in 2023.

The highest female representation in the upper chamber of bicameral parliaments was in Canada, Australia and Bolivia, and the global percentage was a little over half.

Lithuania has the highest female representation of judges in the judicial branch of government, though only a couple dozen countries had data for this measure as of 2023.[260]

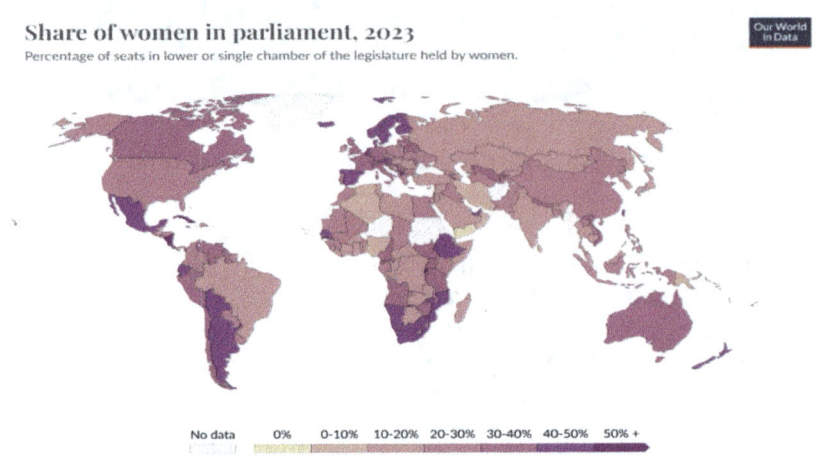

Target 16.8

Broaden and strengthen the participation of developing countries in the institutions of global governance

- Indicator 16.8.1: Proportion of members and voting rights of developing countries in international organizations

Target 16.8 mirrors Target 10.6 in its focus on participation of developing countries in international organisations. Indicator 16.8.1 uses the same institutions as its measure, making its results a duplicate of 10.6.1.

Target 16.9

By 2030, provide legal identity for all, including birth registration

- Indicator 16.9.1: Proportion of children under 5 years of age whose births have been registered with a civil authority, by age

The countries with the lowest rates of registered births as of 2022 were both in the Horn of Africa - Ethiopia and Somalia.[261] Each had less than 6% of births registered with a civil authority, compared to the worldwide share of 72% as of 2018, posing a challenge for the provision of legal identity for all by 2030.

Target 16.10

Ensure public access to information and protect fundamental freedoms, in accordance with national legislation and international agreements

- Indicator 16.10.1: Number of verified cases of killing, kidnapping, enforced disappearance, arbitrary detention and torture of journalists, associated media personnel, trade unionists and human rights advocates in the previous 12 months
- Indicator 16.10.2: Number of countries that adopt and implement constitutional, statutory and/or policy guarantees for public access to information

The number of verified cases of killings of journalists, human rights defenders, and trade unionists was 320 in 2023.[262] In the SDG period so far, this number peaked in 2018 with 476 and was 349 in 2015.

The number of countries which had adopted and implemented access to information laws and policies was 138 as of 2023.[263]

Target 16.A

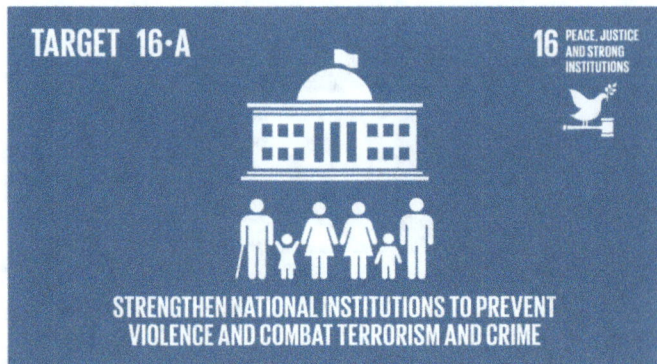

Strengthen relevant national institutions, including through international cooperation, for building capacity at all levels, in particular in developing countries, to prevent violence and combat terrorism and crime

- Indicator 16.a.1: Existence of independent national human rights institutions in compliance with the Paris Principles

The Paris Principles are the basic standards for national human rights institutions, accredited by GANHRI (Global Alliance of National Human Rights Institutions).

The share of countries with such accreditation worldwide is 44% as of 2023, up from 35% in 2015.[264] In the least developed countries, this was 42%, up from 27% since 2015.

Target 16.B

Promote and enforce non-discriminatory laws and policies for sustainable development

- Indicator 16.b.1: Proportion of population reporting having personally felt discriminated against or harassed in the previous 12 months on the basis of a ground of discrimination prohibited under international human rights law

Many countries don't have data for Indicator 16.b.1 as of 2023.[265] Among those who did, the smallest proportion of discrimination reported by adults - each with less than 5% - were in Cuba, Portugal, Belarus and Vietnam.

Goal #17

Strengthen the means of implementation and revitalize the Global Partnership for Sustainable Development

Target 17.1

**Strengthen domestic resource mobilization, including through international support to
developing countries, to improve domestic capacity for tax and other revenue collection**

- Indicator 17.1.1: Total government revenue as a proportion of GDP, by source
- Indicator 17.1.2: Proportion of domestic budget funded by domestic taxes

The country with the highest government revenue as a share of GDP as of 2022 was the island nation of Kiribati (96%), followed by Norway (64%).[266] The lowest shares were in Ethiopia and Sri Lanka, with less than 10%, and the worldwide share was 33%, up a couple percentage points since 2015.

The country with the highest share of its budget funded by taxes in 2022 was Nicaragua (97%).[267] The lowest was Iraq (3%), and the global share was 57%, down a couple percentage points from 2015.

Target 17.2

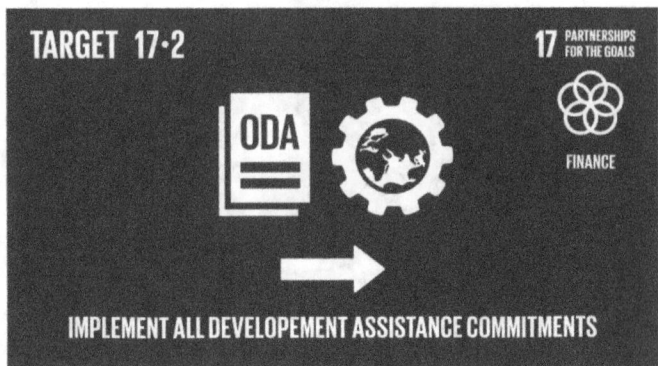

Developed countries to implement fully their official development assistance commitments, including the commitment by many developed countries to achieve the Target of 0.7 per cent of gross national income for official development assistance (ODA/GNI) to developing countries and 0.15 to 0.20 per cent of ODA/GNI to least developed countries; ODA providers are encouraged to consider setting a Target to provide at least 0.20 per cent of ODA/GNI to least developed countries

- Indicator 17.2.1: Net official development assistance, total and to least developed countries, as a proportion of the Organization for Economic Cooperation and Development (OECD) Development Assistance Committee donors' gross national income (GNI)

As of 2023, only five countries have met the aim of 0.7% of GNI to ODA: Luxembourg, Sweden, Norway, Germany, Denmark.[268] Norway, Sweden, and Luxembourg were the only countries, as of 2022, to meet the aim of 0.2% of GNI given as ODA to least developed countries.[269]

Target 17.3

Mobilize additional financial resources for developing countries from multiple sources

- Indicator 17.3.1: Additional financial resources mobilized for developing countries from multiple sources
- Indicator 17.3.2: Volume of remittances (in United States dollars) as a proportion of total GDP

Other than ODA, financial resources for developing countries can include private flows, for example foreign direct investment and trade.

Foreign direct investment inflows were 2.6% of GDP in Sub-Saharan Africa in 2015, peaked at 3.6% in 2021, but dropped to 1.5% in 2022.[270] In South Asia, it started at 1.8% of GDP in 2015, and was 1.25% by 2022, so additional financial resources have not been mobilised overall.

Worldwide, foreign direct investment was 2% of gross world product as of 2022, down a fraction since 2015, but these figures don't suggest investments were to developing countries.

Remittances received affects the balance of payments of developing countries in a positive way. Tajikistan had the highest share of remittances as a proportion of GDP as of 2022, occupying half its GDP, and was 2.6% in Sub-Saharan Africa, 4% in South Asia, and less than 1% worldwide.[271]

Target 17.4

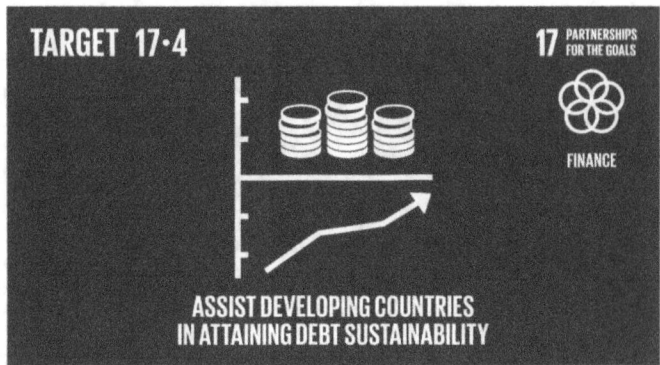

Assist developing countries in attaining long-term debt sustainability through coordinated policies aimed at fostering debt financing, debt relief and debt restructuring, as appropriate, and address the external debt of highly indebted poor countries to reduce debt distress

- Indicator 17.4.1: Debt service as a proportion of exports of goods and services

Countries can enter financial distress when unable to pay their debts, for which there may be a need to restructure for relief.

As of 2022, Pakistan, Guinea-Bissau and Argentina had the largest levels of debt, equal to between a quarter and a third of the value of their goods and services exports.[272] Among the least developed countries, the proportion was 8%, up from 7% in 2015.

Target 17.5

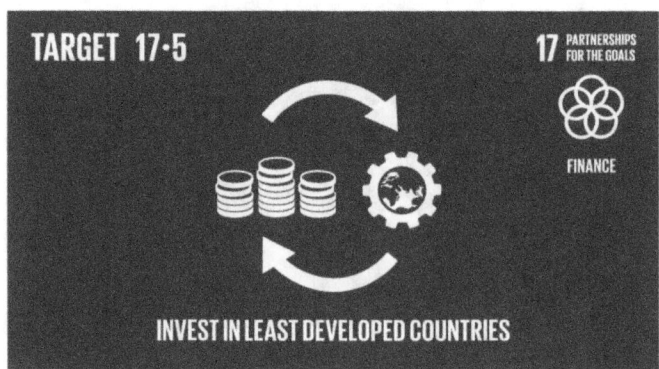

Adopt and implement investment promotion regimes for least developed countries

- Indicator 17.5.1: Number of countries that adopt and implement investment promotion regimes for developing countries, including the least developed countries

The estimated financing gap for the achievement of the SDGs for developing countries is $2.5 trillion, yet where is this investment to come from?[273] Where are the least developed countries to get advice on what policies will promote investment?

As of 2021, 183 countries have signed an investment promotion treaty with developing countries - among these, 120 with least developed countries.[274]

Target 17.6

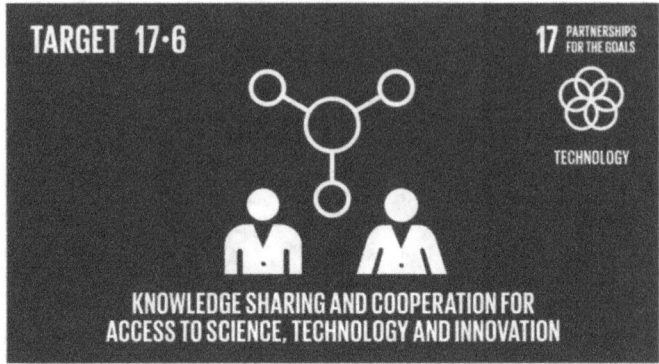

Enhance North-South, South-South and triangular regional and international cooperation on and access to science, technology and innovation and enhance knowledge-sharing on mutually agreed terms, including through improved coordination among existing mechanisms, in particular at the United Nations level, and through a global technology facilitation mechanism

- Indicator 17.6.1: Fixed broadband subscriptions per 100 inhabitants, by speed
-

Worldwide, as of 2022, there were 18 landline internet subscriptions per 100 people, up from 11 in 2015, but less than 5 per 100 people in Sub-Saharan Africa, South and Southeast Asia, and Central America.[275]

Target 17.7

Promote the development, transfer, dissemination and diffusion of environmentally sound technologies to developing countries on favourable terms, including on concessional and preferential terms, as mutually agreed

- Indicator 17.7.1: Total amount of funding for developing countries to promote the development, transfer, dissemination and diffusion of environmentally sound technologies

The world's biggest exporter of 'environmentally sound technologies' is China, which in 2020, exported $258 billion.[276] Worldwide, there were $1.17 trillion of such exports, a similar amount to 2015.

Target 17.8

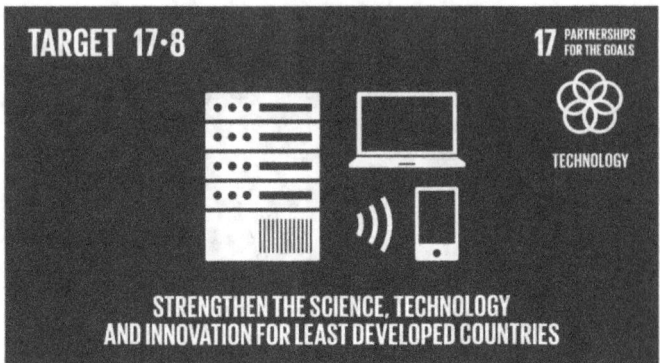

Fully operationalize the technology bank and science, technology and innovation capacity-building mechanism for least developed countries by 2017 and enhance the use of enabling technology, in particular information and communications technology

- Indicator 17.8.1: Proportion of individuals using the Internet

Countries with less than 10% of individuals using the internet as of 2022 were in the Republic of Congo, Kenya, Burundi, and South Sudan.[277] The global share was 63%, up from 40% in 2015, with a 20% share for the low-income countries, up from 9% in 2015.

Target 17.9

Enhance international support for implementing effective and Targeted capacity-building in developing countries to support national plans to implement all the Sustainable Development Goals, including through North-South, South-South and triangular cooperation

- Indicator 17.9.1: Dollar value of financial and technical assistance (including through North-South, South-South and triangular cooperation) committed to developing countries

The countries who'd received over a billion dollars in development cooperation in the form of technical help in 2022 were:

- Mexico
- Egypt
- Bangladesh
- Colombia
- India
- Indonesia
- Philippines[278]

Ukraine received $11 billion due to the war there.

Asia and Africa received $13 billion in 2022, Latin America and the Caribbean $8 billion, and the least developed countries $9 billion. Each of these regions saw an increase of annual technical help equal to a couple billion dollars over the SDG period. The exception was Asia, for which funding was reduced by this amount over the same period.

Target 17.10

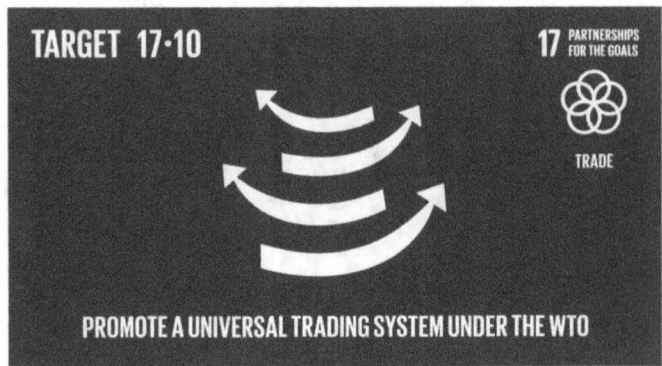

Promote a universal, rules-based, open, non-discriminatory and equitable multilateral trading system under the World Trade Organization, including through the conclusion of negotiations under its Doha Development Agenda

- Indicator 17.10.1: Worldwide weighted tariff-average

Target 17.10 reintroduces the Doha Development Agenda of the World Trade Organization, already explored in several previous Targets.

Worldwide, the average tariffs across all products as of 2017 was 2%, a fraction less than at the adoption of the SDGs in 2015.[279]

Target 17.11

Significantly increase the exports of developing countries, in particular with a view to doubling the least developed countries' share of global exports by 2020

- Indicator 17.11.1: Developing countries' and least developed countries' share of global exports

As of 2023, developing countries' share of global exports was 47%, with only a 2% increase since 2015, and 1% for least developed countries, which was the same between 2015 and 2020.[280]

Target 17.12

Realize timely implementation of duty-free and quota-free market access on a lasting basis for all least developed countries, consistent with World Trade Organization decisions, including by ensuring that preferential rules of origin applicable to imports from least developed countries are transparent and simple, and contribute to facilitating market access

- Indicator 17.12.1: Weighted average tariffs faced by developing countries, least developed countries and small island developing States

The tariffs faced by low-income countries averaged 10% as of 2017, about the same as at the adoption of the SDGs in 2015, compared to the average world tariff of 2%.[281]

Target 17.13

Enhance global macroeconomic stability, including through policy coordination and policy coherence

- Indicator 17.13.1: Macroeconomic Dashboard

The Macroeconomic Dashboard is a collection of financial and fiscal indicators.

An example of one of these is inflation of consumer prices. The countries with the highest figures for this in 2022 were Zimbabwe and Sudan, each with rates higher than 100.[282] Worldwide, consumer price inflation was 8% in 2022, up from 1% in 2015.

Another measure from the Macroeconomic Dashboard is public sector debt. The highest as of 2021 was Greece, with 207%, though a lot of countries were missing data.[283]

Target 17.14

Enhance policy coherence for sustainable development

- Indicator 17.14.1: Number of countries with mechanisms in place to enhance policy coherence of sustainable development

Policy coherence is an effort to ensure all parts of government are working toward sustainable development.

Few countries have reported data on this Target, but those with a high degree of mechanisms ensuring policy coherence include Colombia and Qatar, each with a perfect score.[284]

Target 17.15

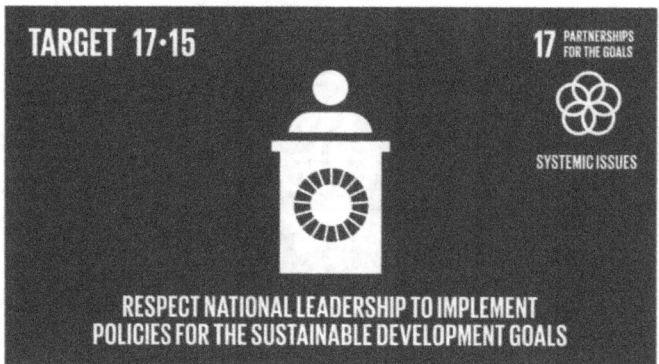

Respect each country's policy space and leadership to establish and implement policies for poverty eradication and sustainable development

- Indicator 17.15.1: Extent of use of country-owned results frameworks and planning tools by providers of development cooperation

Country-owned results frameworks define how countries choose to measure development themselves. For example, a developing country can create a plan for how it intends to reduce poverty over the next 10 years, which donors may consider when providing aid, rather than imposing their own designs on the recipient.

On this measure, providers of development cooperation used 57% of country-owned results frameworks as of 2018.[285]

Target 17.16

Enhance the Global Partnership for Sustainable Development, complemented by multi-stakeholder partnerships that mobilize and share knowledge, expertise, technology and financial resources, to support the achievement of the Sustainable Development Goals in all countries, in particular developing countries

- Indicator 17.16.1: Number of countries reporting progress in multi-stakeholder development effectiveness monitoring frameworks that support the achievement of the sustainable development goals

The Global Partnership for Sustainable Development spells out the essence of SDG #17, calling upon countries to help one another in achieving the SDGs.

As of 2018, 36 countries who were recipients of knowledge in support of the SDGs were reporting progress in such frameworks.[286] 20 of these were least developed countries, and 20 countries were providing such help.

Target 17.17

Encourage and promote effective public, public-private and civil society partnerships, building on the experience and resourcing strategies of partnerships

- Indicator 17.17.1: Amount in United States dollars committed to public-private partnerships for infrastructure

Many of the aims of the SDGs involve infrastructure investments, such as for the energy transition or water provision. Governments can raise some of this money, but often it needs a combination of public and private finance. This is extra difficult when the major credit rating agencies hold unfavourable assessments of the least developed countries, making it more expensive for these governments to finance crucial infrastructure.

Brazil, China, and India each raised more than $5 billion for public-private partnerships in 2020.[287]

Target 17.18

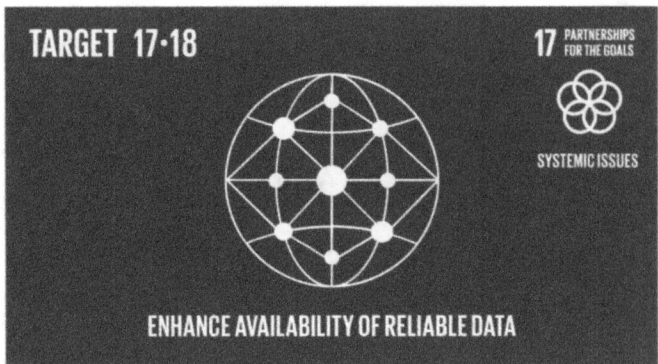

By 2020, enhance capacity-building support to developing countries, including for least developed countries and small island developing States, to increase significantly the availability of high-quality, timely and reliable data disaggregated by income, gender, age, race, ethnicity, migratory status, disability, geographic location and other characteristics relevant in national contexts

- Indicator 17.18.1: Statistical capacity Indicators
- Indicator 17.18.2: Number of countries that have national statistical legislation that complies with the Fundamental Principles of Official Statistics
- Indicator 17.18.3: Number of countries with a national statistical plan that is fully funded and under implementation, by source of funding

Goals give us inspiration. Targets within those goals help break down the vast ambition, and indicators give us tools to measure what we aspire toward. But we need data to inform those indicators, to know how we're progressing toward our goals. For example, how will we know we're lifting the 615 million (as of December 2024) out of extreme poverty, or if there's a reversal, without good data?[288] But many countries are in dire need of development, hampering their capacity to collect data of their citizens. As of 2023, many countries in South America and Africa don't have statistics adherent to the UN Fundamental Principles of data.[289] In an irony, a couple dozen countries don't have data for Indicator 17.8.2.

Target 17.19

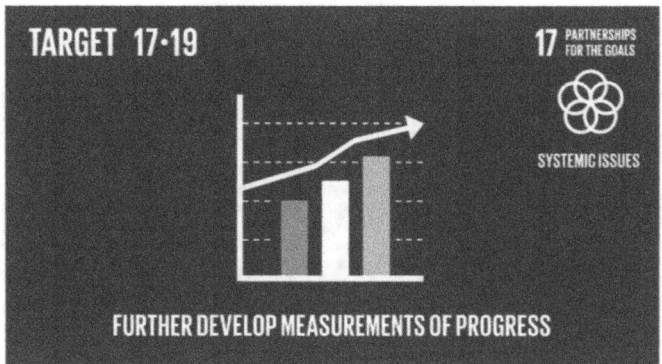

By 2030, build on existing initiatives to develop measurements of progress on sustainable development that complement gross domestic product, and support statistical capacity-building in developing countries

- Indicator 17.19.1: Dollar value of all resources made available to strengthen statistical capacity in developing countries
- Indicator 17.19.2: Proportion of countries that (a) have conducted at least one population and housing census in the last 10 years; and (b) have achieved 100 per cent birth registration and 80 per cent death registration

The most dollars received to strengthen statistical capacity were in several African countries, Vietnam, Serbia and Nepal, which each spent over $10 million toward this in 2020, amongst global spending of $541 million.[290]

As of 2023, only a bit more than a dozen countries hadn't completed a census in the past decade.[291] Several African countries and Afghanistan registered deaths at a rate lower than 10%, and results for the proportion of registered births were explored in Target 16.9.[292]

References

[1] Sachs, J. D., Lafortune, G., & Fuller, G. (2024). *The SDGs and the UN Summit of the Future. Sustainable Development Report 2024*. Paris: SDSN, Dublin: Dublin University Press. 10.25546/108572
[2] Sachs, J., Fajans-Turner, V., Smith, T., Kennedy-Cuomo, C., Parejo, T., & Sam Loni, S. (2018, December). *Closing the SDG Budget Gap by Move Humanity*. https://movehumanity.org/wp-content/uploads/2019/03/PICA-HUMANITY-REPORT-WEB-V7-190319.pdf
[3] UN. (2025). *Ending Poverty | United Nations*. Retrieved January 27, 2025, from https://www.un.org/en/global-issues/ending-poverty
[4] World Data Lab. (2024). World Poverty Clock. Retrieved December 2024, from https://worldpoverty.io/
[5] World Bank. (2018, October 17). *Nearly Half the World Lives on Less than $5.50 a Day*. https://www.worldbank.org/en/news/press-release/2018/10/17/nearly-half-the-world-lives-on-less-than-550-a-day#:~:text=Over%201.9%20billion%20people%2C%20or,less%20than%20%245.50%20a%20day.
[6] "Data Page: Share of population living below national poverty lines". Our World in Data (2025). Data adapted from World Bank. Retrieved from https://ourworldindata.org/grapher/share-of-population-living-in-poverty-by-national-poverty-lines
[7] UN. (2025a). *SDG Indicators*. https://unstats.un.org/sdgs/report/2021/goal-01/
[8] Brecht, H., Deichmann, U., & Gun Wang, H. (2013, June). *A Global Urban Risk Index*. World Bank. https://documents1.worldbank.org/curated/en/804651468331205546/pdf/WPS6506.pdf; IPCC. (2011, November 28). *IPCC Special Report on Managing the Risks of Extreme Events and Disasters to Advance Climate Change Adaptation*. https://www.ipcc.ch/site/assets/uploads/2018/04/SREX_fact_sheet.pdf
[9] OECD. (2025). *Official development assistance (ODA)*. OECD. https://www.oecd.org/en/topics/policy-issues/official-development-assistance-oda.html
[10] UN. (2015). *United Nations Millennium Development Goals*. Retrieved January 27, 2025, from https://www.un.org/millenniumgoals/poverty.shtml
[11] "Data Page: Share of people that are undernourished", part of the following publication: Hannah Ritchie, Pablo Rosado and Max Roser (2023) - "Agricultural Production". Data adapted from Food and Agriculture Organization of the United Nations. Retrieved from https://ourworldindata.org/grapher/prevalence-of-undernourishment [online resource]; UN. (2015). *Goal 2: Zero Hunger - United Nations Sustainable Development*. Retrieved January 27, 2025, from https://www.un.org/sustainabledevelopment/hunger
[12] "Data Page: Share of children who are stunted", part of the following publication: Hannah Ritchie, Pablo Rosado and Max Roser (2023) - "Hunger and Undernourishment". Data adapted from World Health Organization. Retrieved from https://ourworldindata.org/grapher/share-of-children-younger-than-5-who-suffer-from-stunting [online resource]
[13] "Data Page: Malnutrition: Share of children who are wasted". Our World in Data (2025). Data adapted from UNICEF, WHO, World Bank. Retrieved from https://ourworldindata.org/grapher/share-of-children-with-a-weight-too-low-for-their-height-wasting [online resource]; "Data Page: Share of children who are overweight". Our World in Data (2025). Data adapted from World Health Organization, UNICEF and the World Bank. Retrieved from https://ourworldindata.org/grapher/share-of-children-who-are-overweight [online resource]
[14] "Data Page: Agricultural value added per worker". Our World in Data (2025). Data adapted from World Bank based on data from multiple sources. Retrieved from https://ourworldindata.org/grapher/agricultural-value-added-per-worker-wdi
[15] "Data Page: Share of agricultural land being productively and sustainably used". Our World in Data (2025). Data adapted from Food and Agriculture Organization of the United Nations. Retrieved from https://ourworldindata.org/grapher/share-of-agricultural-land-being-productively-and-sustainably-used [online resource]
[16] "Data Page: Number of unique plant genetic samples in conservation facilities". Our World in Data (2025). Data adapted from Food and Agriculture Organization of the United Nations. Retrieved from https://ourworldindata.org/grapher/number-of-accessions-of-plant-genetic-resources-secured-in-conservation-facilities [online resource]
[17] "Data Page: Total financial assistance and flows for agriculture, by recipient". Our World in Data (2025). Data adapted from Organisation for Economic Co-operation and Development. Retrieved from https://ourworldindata.org/grapher/total-financial-assistance-and-flows-for-agriculture-by-recipient [online resource]
[18] "Data Page: Agricultural export subsidies". Our World in Data (2025). Data adapted from World Trade Organization. Retrieved from https://ourworldindata.org/grapher/agricultural-export-subsidies [online resource]
[19] "Data Page: Indicator of food price anomalies". Our World in Data (2025). Data adapted from Food and Agriculture Organization of the United Nations. Retrieved from https://ourworldindata.org/grapher/food-price-anomalies
[20] "Data Page: Maternal mortality ratio". Our World in Data (2025). Data adapted from World Health Organization. Retrieved from https://ourworldindata.org/grapher/maternal-mortality-ratio-who-gho [online resource]
[21] "Data Page: Share of births attended by skilled health staff". Our World in Data (2025). Data adapted from Demographic and Health Surveys (DHS) and UNICEF (via World Bank). Retrieved from https://ourworldindata.org/grapher/births-attended-by-health-staff-sdgs [online resource]
[22] UNICEF. (2024, March). *Under-five mortality*. UNICEF Data. https://data.unicef.org/topic/child-survival/under-five-mortality
[23] "Data Page: Neonatal mortality rate", part of the following publication: Saloni Dattani, Fiona Spooner, Hannah Ritchie and Max Roser (2023) - "Child and Infant Mortality". Data adapted from United Nations Inter-agency Group for Child Mortality Estimation, Various sources. Retrieved from https://ourworldindata.org/grapher/neonatal-mortality-wdi [online resource]| "Data Page: Child mortality rate", part of the following publication: Saloni Dattani, Fiona Spooner, Hannah Ritchie and Max Roser (2023) - "Child and Infant Mortality". Data adapted from United Nations Inter-agency Group for Child Mortality Estimation, Various sources. Retrieved from https://ourworldindata.org/grapher/child-mortality-igme
[24] UNAIDS. (2025). *Global HIV & AIDS statistics — Fact sheet*. UNAIDS. Retrieved January 27, 2025, from https://www.unaids.org/en/resources/fact-sheet
[25] World Health Organization. (2025). *HIV – New HIV infections (per 1000 uninfected population)*. https://www.who.int/data/gho/data/indicators/indicator-details/GHO/new-hiv-infections-(per-1000-uninfected-population)

[26] World Health Organization. (2024, October 29). *Tuberculosis (TB)*. World Health Organization (WHO). Retrieved January 27, 2025, from https://www.who.int/news-room/fact-sheets/detail/tuberculosis
[27] "Data Page: Rate of new tuberculosis cases", part of the following publication: Saloni Dattani, Fiona Spooner, Hannah Ritchie and Max Roser (2023) - "Tuberculosis". Data adapted from WHO, Various sources. Retrieved from https://ourworldindata.org/grapher/incidence-of-tuberculosis-sdgs [online resource]
[28] World Health Organization. (2024, December 11). *Malaria*. World Health Organization. Retrieved January 27, 2025, from https://www.who.int/news-room/fact-sheets/detail/malaria
[29] Our World in Data team (2023) - "Ensure healthy lives and promote well-being for all at all ages" Published online at OurWorldinData.org. Retrieved from: 'https://ourworldindata.org/sdgs/good-health-wellbeing' [Online Resource]
[30] Our World in Data team (2023) - "Ensure healthy lives and promote well-being for all at all ages" Published online at OurWorldinData.org. Retrieved from: 'https://ourworldindata.org/sdgs/good-health-wellbeing' [Online Resource]
[31] "Data Page: Number of people requiring treatment against neglected tropical diseases". Our World in Data (2025). Data adapted from World Health Organization. Retrieved from https://ourworldindata.org/grapher/interventions-ntds-sdgs
[32] World Health Organization. (2015). *Global Health Estimates*. World Health Organization. Retrieved January 27, 2025, from https://www.who.int/data/global-health-estimates
[33] World Bank Group. (2025, Jan 15). *World Development Indicators*. World Bank Group Data Catalog. https://datacatalog.worldbank.org/search/dataset/0037712/World-Development-Indicators
[34] "Data Page: Total alcohol consumption per capita". Our World in Data (2025). Data adapted from World Health Organization (via World Bank). Retrieved from https://ourworldindata.org/grapher/total-alcohol-consumption-per-capita-litres-of-pure-alcohol [online resource]
[35] World Health Organization. (2025). *SDG Target 3.6 Halve the number of global deaths and injuries from road traffic accidents*. Road traffic mortality. https://www.who.int/data/gho/data/themes/topics/sdg-target-3_6-road-traffic-injuries
[36] World Health Organization – processed by Our World in Data. "3.6.1 – Death rate due to road traffic injuries, by sex (per 100,000 population) - SH_STA_TRAF - Both sexes" [dataset]. World Health Organization [original data].
[37] "Data Page: Share of women whose family planning needs are met". Our World in Data (2025). Data adapted from Population Division, Department of Economic and Social Affairs and United Nations Population Fund. Retrieved from https://ourworldindata.org/grapher/share-of-married-women-ages-15-49-years-whose-need-for-family-planning-is-satisfied
[38] "Data Page: Adolescent birth rate, 10-14 year olds". Our World in Data (2025). Data adapted from Population Division, Department of Economic and Social Affairs and United Nations Population Fund. Retrieved from https://ourworldindata.org/grapher/adolescent-fertility [online resource]
[39] World Bank. (2025). Poverty and Inequality Platform. Retrieved January 27, 2025, from https://pip.worldbank.org/home
[40] "Data Page: The Universal Health Coverage (UHC) Service Coverage Index". Our World in Data (2025). Data adapted from World Health Organization. Retrieved from https://ourworldindata.org/grapher/universal-health-coverage-index
[41] "Data Page: Share of population with very large expenditures on health". Our World in Data (2025). Data adapted from World Health Organization and World Bank. Retrieved from https://ourworldindata.org/grapher/large-household-expenditures-health [online resource]; "Data Page: Share of population with large expenditures on health". Our World in Data (2025). Data adapted from World Health Organization and World Bank. Retrieved from https://ourworldindata.org/grapher/share-of-population-with-large-household-expenditures-on-health-10pc
[42] World Health Organization. (2024, October 16). *Household air pollution*. World Health Organization (WHO). Retrieved January 27, 2025, from https://www.who.int/news-room/fact-sheets/detail/household-air-pollution-and-health
[43] World Health Organization – processed by Our World in Data. "3.9.1 - Age-standardized mortality rate attributed to household and ambient air pollution (deaths per 100,000 population) - SH_STA_ASAIRP" [dataset]. World Health Organization, "Global Health Observatory (GHO), World Health Organisation (WHO)" [original data]; "Data Page: Death rate attributable to unsafe water, sanitation, and hygiene". Our World in Data (2025). Data adapted from World Health Organization. Retrieved from https://ourworldindata.org/grapher/mortality-rate-attributable-to-wash [online resource]; "Data Page: Death rate from unintentional poisoning". Our World in Data (2025). Data adapted from World Health Organization. Retrieved from https://ourworldindata.org/grapher/death-rate-from-poisonings [online resource]
[44] "Data Page: Prevalence of current tobacco use (% of adults)". Our World in Data (2025). Data adapted from World Health Organization (via World Bank). Retrieved from https://ourworldindata.org/grapher/share-of-adults-who-smoke
[45] "Data Page: Share of one-year-olds vaccinated against diphtheria, pertussis, and tetanus", part of the following publication: Samantha Vanderslott, Saloni Dattani, Fiona Spooner and Max Roser (2022) - "Vaccination". Data adapted from WHO & UNICEF. Retrieved from https://ourworldindata.org/grapher/share-of-children-immunized-dtp3
[46] "Data Page: Share of children fully vaccinated against measles", part of the following publication: Samantha Vanderslott, Saloni Dattani, Fiona Spooner and Max Roser (2022) – "Vaccination". Data adapted from WHO & UNICEF. Retrieved from https://ourworldindata.org/grapher/share-of-children-vaccinated-with-mcv2 [online resource]
[47] "Data Page: Share of one-year-olds vaccinated against Streptococcus pneumoniae", part of the following publication: Samantha Vanderslott, Saloni Dattani, Fiona Spooner and Max Roser (2022) - "Vaccination". Data adapted from WHO & UNICEF. Retrieved from https://ourworldindata.org/grapher/share-of-one-year-olds-who-received-the-final-dose-of-pneumococcal-vaccine [online resource]
[48] "Data Page: Net official development assistance to medical research and basic health sectors". Our World in Data (2025). Data adapted from Organisation for Economic Co-operation and Development. Retrieved from https://ourworldindata.org/grapher/net-oda-to-medical-research [online resource]
[49] World Health Organization. (2025). *Medical doctors (per 10 000 population)*. World Health Organization (WHO). Retrieved January 27, 2025, from https://www.who.int/data/gho/data/indicators/indicator-details/GHO/medical-doctors-(per-10-000-population)
[50] World Health Organization. (2025). *Strengthening global health security at the human-animal interface - Strengthening global health security at the human-animal interface*. World Health Organization. Retrieved January 27, 2025, from https://www.who.int/activities/strengthening-global-health-security-at-the-human-animal-interface
[51] World Health Organization – processed by Our World in Data. "Chemical events" [dataset]. World Health Organization, "IHR State Party Self-assessment annual report received and recorded in the WHO e-SPAR Platform (https://extranet.who.int/e-spar/)." [original data].
[52] "Data Page: Share of S. aureus infections resistant to methicillin". Our World in Data (2025). Data adapted from World Health Organization. Retrieved from https://ourworldindata.org/grapher/share-of-s-aureus-bloodstream-infections-that-are-resistant-to-antibiotics [online resource]; "Data Page: Share of E. coli infections resistant to cephalosporins". Our World in

Data (2025). Data adapted from World Health Organization. Retrieved from https://ourworldindata.org/grapher/share-of-e-coli-bloodstream-infections-due-to-antimicrobial-resistant-bacteria [online resource]

[53] "Data Page: Completion rate of primary education". Our World in Data (2025). Data adapted from UNESCO Institute for Statistics. Retrieved from https://ourworldindata.org/grapher/completion-rate-of-primary-education [online resource]

[54] "Data Page: Completion rate of lower-secondary education". Our World in Data (2025). Data adapted from UNESCO Institute for Statistics. Retrieved from https://ourworldindata.org/grapher/completion-rate-of-lower-secondary-education

[55] "Data Page: Completion rate of upper-secondary education". Our World in Data (2025). Data adapted from UNESCO Institute for Statistics. Retrieved from https://ourworldindata.org/grapher/completion-rate-of-upper-secondary-education-sdg

[56] "Data Page: Proportion of children aged 3-5 years who are developmentally on track". Our World in Data (2025). Data adapted from UNICEF. Retrieved from https://ourworldindata.org/grapher/proportion-of-children-developmentally-on-track

[57] "Data Page: Net enrolment rate, pre-primary, both sexes". Our World in Data (2025). Data adapted from UNESCO Institute for Statistics. Retrieved from https://ourworldindata.org/grapher/net-enrollment-rate-pre-primary [online resource]

[58] UNESCO Institute for Statistics – processed by Our World in Data. "Net enrollment rate, pre-primary, boys (%)" [dataset]. UNESCO Institute for Statistics, "Data from multiple sources" [original data].

[59] "Data Page: Gross enrolment ratio in tertiary education". Our World in Data (2025). Data adapted from UNESCO Institute for Statistics. Retrieved from https://ourworldindata.org/grapher/gross-enrollment-ratio-in-tertiary-education

[60] "Data Page: Primary school completion rates, adjusted gender parity index". Our World in Data (2025). Data adapted from UNESCO Institute for Statistics. Retrieved from https://ourworldindata.org/grapher/primary-completion-rate-adjusted-gender-parity-index [online resource]

[61] "Data Page: Lower-secondary school completion rates, adjusted gender parity index". Our World in Data (2025). Data adapted from UNESCO Institute for Statistics. Retrieved from https://ourworldindata.org/grapher/lower-secondary-completion-rate-adjusted-gender-parity-index [online resource]

[62] Multiple sources compiled by World Bank (2024) – processed by Our World in Data. "Females" [dataset]. UNESCO Institute for Statistics, "World Development Indicators" [original data].

[63] "Data Page: Literacy rate in adult men". Our World in Data (2025). Data adapted from UNESCO Institute for Statistics. Retrieved from https://ourworldindata.org/grapher/adult-literacy-male [online resource]; "Data Page: Literacy rate in adult women". Our World in Data (2025). Data adapted from UNESCO Institute for Statistics. Retrieved from https://ourworldindata.org/grapher/adult-literacy-female [online resource]

[64] "Data Page: Mainstreaming of global citizenship and sustainable development into national education policies". Our World in Data (2025). Data adapted from Data from multiple sources compiled by the UN. Retrieved from https://ourworldindata.org/grapher/mainstreaming-sustainable-development-into-national-education-policies [online resource]; "Data Page: Mainstreaming of global citizenship and sustainable development into curricula". Our World in Data (2025). Data adapted from Data from multiple sources compiled by the UN. Retrieved from https://ourworldindata.org/grapher/mainstreaming-sustainable-development-into-curricula [online resource]; "Data Page: Mainstreaming of global citizenship and sustainable development into teacher education". Our World in Data (2025). Data adapted from Data from multiple sources compiled by the UN. Retrieved from https://ourworldindata.org/grapher/mainstreaming-sustainable-development-into-teacher-education [online resource]; "Data Page: Mainstreaming of global citizenship and sustainable development into student assessment". Our World in Data (2025). Data adapted from Data from multiple sources compiled by the UN. Retrieved from https://ourworldindata.org/grapher/mainstreaming-sustainable-development-into-student-assessment [online resource]

[65] UNESCO Institute for Statistics – processed by Our World in Data. "Lower secondary" [dataset]. UNESCO Institute for Statistics, "Data from multiple sources" [original data]; UNESCO Institute for Statistics – processed by Our World in Data. "Lower secondary" [dataset]. UNESCO Institute for Statistics, "Data from multiple sources" [original data].

[66] UNESCO Institute for Statistics – processed by Our World in Data. "Lower secondary" [dataset]. UNESCO Institute for Statistics, "Data from multiple sources" [original data].

[67] "Data Page: Share of primary schools with access to the Internet for teaching". Our World in Data (2025). Data adapted from UNESCO Institute for Statistics. Retrieved from https://ourworldindata.org/grapher/primary-schools-with-access-to-internet [online resource]

[68] UNESCO Institute for Statistics – processed by Our World in Data. "Lower secondary" [dataset]. UNESCO Institute for Statistics, "Data from multiple sources" [original data].

[69] "Data Page: Gross overseas development assistance from all donors for scholarships". Our World in Data (2025). Data adapted from Organisation for Economic Co-operation and Development. Retrieved from https://ourworldindata.org/grapher/oda-for-scholarships [online resource]

[70] "Data Page: Percentage of teachers in pre-primary education who are qualified". Our World in Data (2025). Data adapted from UNESCO Institute for Statistics. Retrieved from https://ourworldindata.org/grapher/percentage-of-teachers-in-pre-primary-education-who-are-qualified [online resource]

[71] "Data Page: Percentage of teachers in primary education who are qualified". Our World in Data (2025). Data adapted from UNESCO Institute for Statistics. Retrieved from https://ourworldindata.org/grapher/percentage-of-teachers-in-primary-education-who-are-qualified [online resource]

[72] "Data Page: Percentage of teachers in lower-secondary education who are qualified". Our World in Data (2025). Data adapted from UNESCO Institute for Statistics. Retrieved from https://ourworldindata.org/grapher/percentage-of-teachers-in-lower-secondary-education-who-are-qualified [online resource]

[73] "Data Page: Percentage of teachers in upper-secondary education who are qualified". Our World in Data (2025). Data adapted from UNESCO Institute for Statistics. Retrieved from https://ourworldindata.org/grapher/percentage-of-teachers-in-upper-secondary-education-who-are-qualified [online resource]

[74] "Data Page: Legal frameworks addressing gender equality overall". Our World in Data (2025). Data adapted from UN Women. Retrieved from https://ourworldindata.org/grapher/overarching-legal-frameworks-regarding-gender-equality

[75] "Data Page: Legal frameworks addressing violence against women". Our World in Data (2025). Data adapted from UN Women. Retrieved from https://ourworldindata.org/grapher/legal-frameworks-regarding-violence-against-women

[76] "Data Page: Legal frameworks addressing gender equality in employment and economic benefits". Our World in Data (2025). Data adapted from UN Women. Retrieved from https://ourworldindata.org/grapher/legal-frameworks-addressing-gender-equality-in-employment-and-economic-benefits [online resource]; "Data Page: Legal frameworks addressing

gender equality within marriage and family". Our World in Data (2025). Data adapted from UN Women. Retrieved from https://ourworldindata.org/grapher/legal-frameworks-gender-equality-within-marriage-and-family [online resource]

[77] OHCHR. (2014). OHCHR Dashboard. Retrieved January 27, 2025, from https://indicators.ohchr.org/

[78] "Data Page: Share of women who experienced violence from an intimate partner". Our World in Data (2025). Data adapted from Data from multiple sources compiled by the UN. Retrieved from https://ourworldindata.org/grapher/share-of-women-who-experienced-violence-by-an-intimate-partner-un [online resource]

[79] "Data Page: Share of women who were married by age 15". Our World in Data (2025). Data adapted from UNICEF. Retrieved from https://ourworldindata.org/grapher/women-married-by-age-15 [online resource]

[80] World Health Organization. (2024, February 5). *Female genital mutilation*. World Health Organization. Retrieved January 27, 2025, from https://www.who.int/news-room/fact-sheets/detail/female-genital-mutilation

[81] "Data Page: Prevalence of female genital mutilation". Our World in Data (2025). Data adapted from Data compiled from multiple sources by World Bank. Retrieved from https://ourworldindata.org/grapher/female-genital-mutilation-prevalence

[82] UN Statistics Division and UN WOMEN – processed by Our World in Data. "Women (% of 24 hour day)" [dataset]. UN Statistics Division and UN WOMEN, "Data from multiple sources" [original data].

[83] UN Statistics Division and UN WOMEN – processed by Our World in Data. "Rural men" [dataset]. UN Statistics Division and UN WOMEN, "Data from multiple sources" [original data].

[84] UN Women. (2025). Women in Local Government | Global overview. Retrieved January 27, 2025, from https://localgov.unwomen.org/

[85] "Data Page: Lower chamber female legislators", part of the following publication: Bastian Herre, Lucas Rodés-Guirao and Esteban Ortiz-Ospina (2013) - "Democracy". Data adapted from V-Dem. Retrieved from https://ourworldindata.org/grapher/share-of-women-in-parliament [online resource]

[86] "Data Page: Share of women in local government". Our World in Data (2025). Data adapted from Inter-Parliamentary Union. Retrieved from https://ourworldindata.org/grapher/share-of-women-in-local-government [online resource]

[87] "Data Page: Share of senior and middle management positions filled by women". Our World in Data (2025). Data adapted from International Labour Organization. Retrieved from https://ourworldindata.org/grapher/proportion-of-women-in-senior-and-middle-management-positions [online resource]

[88] "Data Page: Share of firms with a female top manager". Our World in Data (2025). Data adapted from World Bank - Women, Business and the Law. Retrieved from https://ourworldindata.org/grapher/share-firms-top-female-manager

[89] "Data Page: Women who make their own informed decisions regarding sexual relations, contraceptive use and reproductive health care". Our World in Data (2025). Data adapted from United Nations Population Fund. Retrieved from https://ourworldindata.org/grapher/women-informed-decisions-health-sexual-relations [online resource]

[90] "Data Page: Access to sexual and reproductive health care". Our World in Data (2025). Data adapted from United Nations Population Fund. Retrieved from https://ourworldindata.org/grapher/access-to-sexual-health-care-and-education

[91] Food and Agriculture Organization of the United Nations – processed by Our World in Data. "Male population with agricultural land rights" [dataset]. Food and Agriculture Organization of the United Nations, "Data from multiple sources" [original data]; "Data Page: Share of agricultural landowners who are women". Our World in Data (2025). Data adapted from Food and Agriculture Organization of the United Nations. Retrieved from https://ourworldindata.org/grapher/share-of-agricultural-land-owners-that-are-women [online resource]

[92] "Data Page: Equal rights to land ownership". Our World in Data (2025). Data adapted from Food and Agriculture Organization of the United Nations. Retrieved from https://ourworldindata.org/grapher/degree-to-which-the-legal-framework-guarantees-womens-equal-rights-to-land-ownership-andor-control [online resource]

[93] International Telecommunication Union – processed by Our World in Data. "Female phone ownership (%)" [dataset]. International Telecommunication Union, "Data from multiple sources" [original data].

[94] "Data Page: Systems tracking and making public allocations for gender equality and women's empowerment". Our World in Data (2025). Data adapted from Data from multiple sources compiled by the UN. Retrieved from https://ourworldindata.org/grapher/systems-track-gender-equality [online resource]

[95] UN. (2025). *Goal 6 | Department of Economic and Social Affairs*. Sustainable Development Goals. Retrieved January 27, 2025, from https://sdgs.un.org/goals/goal6

[96] "Data Page: Share using safely managed drinking water", part of the following publication: Hannah Ritchie, Fiona Spooner and Max Roser (2021) - "Clean Water and Sanitation". Data adapted from WHO/UNICEF Joint Monitoring Programme for Water Supply, Sanitation and Hygiene (JMP). Retrieved from https://ourworldindata.org/grapher/proportion-using-safely-managed-drinking-water [online resource]

[97] WHO/UNICEF Joint Monitoring Programme for Water Supply, Sanitation and Hygiene (JMP) (2024) – with major processing by Our World in Data

[98] "Data Page: Share of the population using safely managed sanitation facilities", part of the following publication: Hannah Ritchie, Fiona Spooner and Max Roser (2021) - "Clean Water and Sanitation". Data adapted from WHO/UNICEF Joint Monitoring Programme for Water Supply, Sanitation and Hygiene (JMP). Retrieved from https://ourworldindata.org/grapher/share-using-safely-managed-sanitation [online resource]; WHO/UNICEF Joint Monitoring Programme for Water Supply, Sanitation and Hygiene (JMP) (2024) – with major processing by Our World in Data. "Share of the population with access to a handwashing facility with soap and water at home (basic hygiene service) - Residence: Total" [dataset]. WHO/UNICEF Joint Monitoring Programme for Water Supply, Sanitation and Hygiene (JMP), "WHO/UNICEF Joint Monitoring Programme for Water Supply, Sanitation and Hygiene (JMP) - Households"; WHO/UNICEF Joint Monitoring Programme for Water Supply, Sanitation and Hygiene (JMP), "WHO/UNICEF Joint Monitoring Programme for Water Supply, Sanitation and Hygiene (JMP) - Households - Regions" [original data].

[99] "Data Page: Share of domestic wastewater that is safely treated". Our World in Data (2025). Data adapted from United Nations Human Settlements Programme, World Health Organization and United Nations Statistics Division. Retrieved from https://ourworldindata.org/grapher/wastewater-safely-treated [online resource]

[100] United Nations Environment Programme – processed by Our World in Data. "All water bodies" [dataset]. United Nations Environment Programme, "Data from multiple sources" [original data].

[101] "Data Page: Water productivity, GDP per cubic meter of freshwater withdrawal". Our World in Data (2025). Data adapted from Data compiled from multiple sources by World Bank. Retrieved from https://ourworldindata.org/grapher/water-productivity [online resource]

[102] "Data Page: Water productivity, GDP per cubic meter of freshwater withdrawal". Our World in Data (2025). Data adapted from Data compiled from multiple sources by World Bank. Retrieved from https://ourworldindata.org/grapher/water-productivity [online resource]
[103] World Bank Group. (2025). *Renewable internal freshwater resources, total (billion cubic meters)*. World Bank Group. https://data.worldbank.org/indicator/ER.H2O.INTR.K3; World Bank Group. (2025). *Annual freshwater withdrawals, total (billion cubic meters)*. World Bank Group Data. https://data.worldbank.org/indicator/ER.H2O.FWTL.K3
[104] "Data Page: Freshwater withdrawals as a share of internal resources". Our World in Data (2025). Data adapted from Food and Agriculture Organization of the United Nations. Retrieved from https://ourworldindata.org/grapher/freshwater-withdrawals-as-a-share-of-internal-resources [online resource]
[105] "Data Page: Freshwater withdrawals as a share of internal resources". Our World in Data (2025). Data adapted from Food and Agriculture Organization of the United Nations. Retrieved from https://ourworldindata.org/grapher/freshwater-withdrawals-as-a-share-of-internal-resources [online resource]
[106] "Data Page: Implementation of integrated water resource management". Our World in Data (2025). Data adapted from United Nations Environment Programme. Retrieved from https://ourworldindata.org/grapher/implementation-of-integrated-water-resource-management [online resource]
[107] Intergovernmental Hydrological Programme of UNESCO and United Nations Economic Commission for Europe – processed by Our World in Data. "All basins (rivers, lakes & aquifers)" [dataset]. Intergovernmental Hydrological Programme of UNESCO and United Nations Economic Commission for Europe, "Values aggregated by custodian agencies, Source: Relevant country authority;" [original data].
[108] Ramsar Convention Secretariat. (n.d.). *State of the World's Wetlands and their Services to People: A compilation of recent analyses*. https://www.ramsar.org/sites/default/files/documents/library/strp19_4_bn7_e.pdf; Convention on Wetlands Secretariat. (2020). *A new toolkit for National Wetlands Inventories*. https://www.ramsar.org/sites/default/files/documents/library/nwi_toolkit_2020_e.pdf
[109] "Data Page: Share of land covered by lakes and rivers". Our World in Data (2025). Data adapted from UN Environment Programme. Retrieved from https://ourworldindata.org/grapher/share-of-land-covered-by-lakes-and-rivers
[110] "Data Page: Coverage of wetlands". Our World in Data (2025). Data adapted from UN Environment Programme. Retrieved from https://ourworldindata.org/grapher/coverage-of-wetlands [online resource]
[111] "Data Page: Total official financial flows for water supply and sanitation, by recipient". Our World in Data (2025). Data adapted from Organisation for Economic Co-operation and Development. Retrieved from https://ourworldindata.org/grapher/total-oda-for-water-supply-and-sanitation-by-recipient [online resource]
[112] "Data Page: Total official financial flows for water supply and sanitation, by recipient". Our World in Data (2025). Data adapted from Organisation for Economic Co-operation and Development. Retrieved from https://ourworldindata.org/grapher/total-oda-for-water-supply-and-sanitation-by-recipient [online resource]
[113] "Data Page: Share of countries with procedures for community participation in water and sanitation management". Our World in Data (2025). Data adapted from World Health Organization. Retrieved from https://ourworldindata.org/grapher/share-of-countries-with-procedures-for-community-participation-in-water-sanitation-management [online resource]
[114] "Data Page: Share of the population with access to electricity", part of the following publication: Hannah Ritchie, Pablo Rosado and Max Roser (2019) - "Access to Energy". Data adapted from World Bank. Retrieved from https://ourworldindata.org/grapher/share-of-the-population-with-access-to-electricity [online resource]
[115] "Data Page: Share of the population with access to clean fuels for cooking", part of the following publication: Esteban Ortiz-Ospina and Max Roser (2016) - "Global Health". Data adapted from World Health Organization. Retrieved from https://ourworldindata.org/grapher/access-to-clean-fuels-and-technologies-for-cooking [online resource]
[116] "Data Page: Share of final energy use that comes from renewable sources". Our World in Data (2025). Data adapted from International Energy Agency, International Renewable Energy Agency and United Nations Statistics Division. Retrieved from https://ourworldindata.org/grapher/share-of-final-energy-consumption-from-renewable-sources
[117] UN. (2025). *Goal 7 | Department of Economic and Social Affairs*. Sustainable Development Goals. Retrieved January 27, 2025, from https://sdgs.un.org/goals/goal7
[118] UN. (2025). *Goal 7 | Department of Economic and Social Affairs*. Sustainable Development Goals. Retrieved January 27, 2025, from https://sdgs.un.org/goals/goal7
[119] "Data Page: Energy intensity". Our World in Data (2025). Data adapted from World Bank and International Energy Agency. Retrieved from https://ourworldindata.org/grapher/energy-intensity-of-economies [online resource]
[120] International Energy Agency. (2022). *Key highlights on SDG 7 targets – Tracking SDG7: The Energy Progress Report, 2022 – Analysis - IEA*. International Energy Agency. Retrieved January 27, 2025, from https://www.iea.org/reports/tracking-sdg7-the-energy-progress-report-2022/key-highlights-on-sdg-7-targets
[121] "Data Page: International finance received for clean energy". Our World in Data (2025). Data adapted from Data from multiple sources compiled by the UN. Retrieved from https://ourworldindata.org/grapher/international-finance-clean-energy [online resource]
[122] "Data Page: Renewable electricity-generating capacity per person". Our World in Data (2025). Data adapted from International Renewable Energy Agency and United Nations World Population Prospects. Retrieved from https://ourworldindata.org/grapher/renewable-electricity-generating-capacity-per-capita [online resource]
[123] "Data Page: Annual growth of GDP per capita", part of the following publication: Max Roser, Pablo Arriagada, Joe Hasell, Hannah Ritchie and Esteban Ortiz-Ospina (2023) - "Economic Growth". Data adapted from World Bank and OECD. Retrieved from https://ourworldindata.org/grapher/gdp-per-capita-growth [online resource]
[124] "Data Page: Annual growth of GDP per capita", part of the following publication: Max Roser, Pablo Arriagada, Joe Hasell, Hannah Ritchie and Esteban Ortiz-Ospina (2023) - "Economic Growth". Data adapted from World Bank and OECD. Retrieved from https://ourworldindata.org/grapher/gdp-per-capita-growth [online resource]
[125] "Data Page: Annual growth of GDP per employed person". Our World in Data (2025). Data adapted from International Labour Organisation. Retrieved from https://ourworldindata.org/grapher/growth-rate-of-real-gdp-per-employed-person
[126] "Data Page: Share of workers informally employed in non-agricultural workplaces". Our World in Data (2025). Data adapted from International Labour Organization. Retrieved from https://ourworldindata.org/grapher/informal-employment-of-total-non-agricultural-employment [online resource]
[127] "Data Page: Share of informal employment in agriculture". Our World in Data (2025). Data adapted from International Labour Organization. Retrieved from https://ourworldindata.org/grapher/informal-employment-in-agriculture

[128] International Labour Organization – processed by Our World in Data. "Female" [dataset]. International Labour Organization, "Data from multiple sources" [original data].
[129] "Data Page: Domestic material consumption per capita". Our World in Data (2025). Data adapted from United Nations Environment Programme. Retrieved from https://ourworldindata.org/grapher/domestic-material-consumption-per-capita
[130] "Data Page: Domestic material consumption per gross domestic product". Our World in Data (2025). Data adapted from United Nations Environment Programme. Retrieved from https://ourworldindata.org/grapher/domestic-material-consumption-per-unit-of-gdp [online resource]
[131] "Data Page: Domestic material consumption per gross domestic product". Our World in Data (2025). Data adapted from United Nations Environment Programme. Retrieved from https://ourworldindata.org/grapher/domestic-material-consumption-per-unit-of-gdp [online resource]
[132] "Data Page: Domestic material consumption per capita". Our World in Data (2025). Data adapted from United Nations Environment Programme. Retrieved from https://ourworldindata.org/grapher/domestic-material-consumption-per-capita
[133] ILOSTAT Earnings and labour cost: Average hourly earnings of employees, men (constant 2011 PPP $) – processed by Our World in Data
[134] "Data Page: Unemployment rate". Our World in Data (2025). Data adapted from International Labour Organization. Retrieved from https://ourworldindata.org/grapher/unemployment-rate [online resource]
[135] "Data Page: Share of young people not in education, employment or training". Our World in Data (2025). Data adapted from International Labour Organization. Retrieved from https://ourworldindata.org/grapher/youth-not-in-education-employment-training [online resource]
[136] UN. (2025). *Goal 8 | Department of Economic and Social Affairs*. Sustainable Development Goals. Retrieved January 27, 2025, from https://sdgs.un.org/goals/goal8
[137] "Data Page: Share of young people not in education, employment or training". Our World in Data (2025). Data adapted from International Labour Organization. Retrieved from https://ourworldindata.org/grapher/youth-not-in-education-employment-training [online resource]
[138] UNICEF. (2021, June 9). *Child Labour: Global estimates 2020, trends and the road forward - UNICEF DATA*. UNICEF Data. Retrieved January 27, 2025, from https://data.unicef.org/resources/child-labour-2020-global-estimates-trends-and-the-road-forward/
[139] Walk Free. (2025). *Global findings*. Walk Free. Retrieved January 27, 2025, from https://www.walkfree.org/global-slavery-index/findings/global-findings/
[140] "Data Page: Share of children engaged in labor". Our World in Data (2025). Data adapted from UNICEF and International Labour Organization. Retrieved from https://ourworldindata.org/grapher/children-aged-5-17-engaged-in-labor
[141] UNICEF and International Labour Organization – processed by Our World in Data. "Share of girls engaged in labor" [dataset]. UNICEF and International Labour Organization, "Data from multiple sources" [original data].
[142] "Data Page: Fatal occupational injury rates". Our World in Data (2025). Data adapted from International Labour Organization. Retrieved from https://ourworldindata.org/grapher/fatal-occupational-injuries-among-employees
[143] "Data Page: Non-fatal occupational injury rates". Our World in Data (2025). Data adapted from International Labour Organization. Retrieved from https://ourworldindata.org/grapher/non-fatal-occupational-injuries-per-100000
[144] "Data Page: Level of national compliance with labor rights". Our World in Data (2025). Data adapted from International Labour Organization. Retrieved from https://ourworldindata.org/grapher/level-of-national-compliance-with-labor-rights]
[145] "Data Page: Level of national compliance with labor rights". Our World in Data (2025). Data adapted from International Labour Organization. Retrieved from https://ourworldindata.org/grapher/level-of-national-compliance-with-labor-rights
[146] "Data Page: Share of GDP from tourism", part of the following publication: Bastian Herre and Veronika Samborska (2023) - "Tourism". Data adapted from UNWTO. Retrieved from https://ourworldindata.org/grapher/tourism-gdp-proportion-of-total-gdp [online resource]
[147] "Data Page: Commercial bank branches". Our World in Data (2025). Data adapted from International Monetary Fund (via World Bank). Retrieved from https://ourworldindata.org/grapher/number-of-commercial-bank-branches-per-100000-adults [online resource]
[148] "Data Page: Automated teller machines (ATMs)". Our World in Data (2025). Data adapted from International Monetary Fund (via World Bank). Retrieved from https://ourworldindata.org/grapher/automated-teller-machines-atms-per-100000-adults [online resource]
[149] "Data Page: Share of adults with an account at a financial institution". Our World in Data (2025). Data adapted from World Bank. Retrieved from https://ourworldindata.org/grapher/account-at-financial-institution [online resource]
[150] "Data Page: Total official flows commitments for aid for trade, by recipient". Our World in Data (2025). Data adapted from Organisation for Economic Co-operation and Development. Retrieved from https://ourworldindata.org/grapher/total-oda-for-aid-for-trade-by-recipient [online resource]
[151] "Data Page: Total official flows commitments for aid for trade, by donor". Our World in Data (2025). Data adapted from Organisation for Economic Co-operation and Development. Retrieved from https://ourworldindata.org/grapher/total-oda-for-aid-for-trade-by-donor [online resource]
[152] "Data Page: Existence of a national strategy for youth employment". Our World in Data (2025). Data adapted from International Labour Organisation. Retrieved from https://ourworldindata.org/grapher/national-strategy-for-youth-employment [online resource]
[153] "Data Page: Share of the rural population living near a road". Our World in Data (2025). Data adapted from World Bank. Retrieved from https://ourworldindata.org/grapher/share-of-rural-population-near-a-road [online resource]
[154] "Data Page: Passenger-kilometers by rail". Our World in Data (2025). Data adapted from International Union of Railways. Retrieved from https://ourworldindata.org/grapher/railways-passengers-carried-passenger-km [online resource]
[155] "Data Page: Passenger-kilometers by air". Our World in Data (2025). Data adapted from International Civil Aviation Organization, International Transport Forum and United Nations Conference on Trade and Development. Retrieved from https://ourworldindata.org/grapher/air-passenger-kilometers [online resource]
[156] "Data Page: Tonne-kilometers of air freight". Our World in Data (2025). Data adapted from International Civil Aviation Organization (via World Bank). Retrieved from https://ourworldindata.org/grapher/air-transport-freight-ton-km
[157] "Data Page: Share of manufacturing in gross domestic product (GDP)". Our World in Data (2025). Data adapted from World Bank and OECD. Retrieved from https://ourworldindata.org/grapher/manufacturing-value-added-to-gdp

[158] "Data Page: Manufacturing jobs as a share of total employment". Our World in Data (2025). Data adapted from United Nations Industrial Development Organization and International Labour Organization. Retrieved from https://ourworldindata.org/grapher/manufacturing-share-of-total-employment [online resource]
[159] "Data Page: Manufacturing jobs as a share of total employment". Our World in Data (2025). Data adapted from United Nations Industrial Development Organization and International Labour Organization. Retrieved from https://ourworldindata.org/grapher/manufacturing-share-of-total-employment [online resource]
[160] "Data Page: Share of small-scale manufacturing in total manufacturing". Our World in Data (2025). Data adapted from United Nations Industrial Development Organization. Retrieved from https://ourworldindata.org/grapher/small-scale-industries-share [online resource]
[161] "Data Page: Share of small-scale industries with a loan or line of credit". Our World in Data (2025). Data adapted from World Bank. Retrieved from https://ourworldindata.org/grapher/smalsmall-scale-industries-loan [online resource]
[162] "Data Page: Carbon intensity: CO_2 emissions per dollar of GDP", part of the following publication: Hannah Ritchie, Pablo Rosado and Max Roser (2023) - "CO_2 and Greenhouse Gas Emissions". Data adapted from Global Carbon Project, Bolt and van Zanden. Retrieved from https://ourworldindata.org/grapher/co2-intensity [online resource]
[163] UN. (2025). *Goal 9 | Department of Economic and Social Affairs*. Sustainable Development Goals. Retrieved January 27, 2025, from https://sdgs.un.org/goals/goal9
[164] "Data Page: Research & development spending as a share of GDP". Our World in Data (2025). Data adapted from UNESCO Institute for Statistics. Retrieved from https://ourworldindata.org/grapher/research-spending-gdp
[165] "Data Page: Number of R&D researchers per million people". Our World in Data (2025). Data adapted from UNESCO Institute for Statistics. Retrieved from https://ourworldindata.org/grapher/researchers-in-rd-per-million-people
[166] "Data Page: International financial support to infrastructure". Our World in Data (2025). Data adapted from Organisation for Economic Co-operation and Development. Retrieved from https://ourworldindata.org/grapher/total-oda-for-infrastructure-by-recipient [online resource]
[167] "Data Page: Share of medium and high-tech manufacturing in gross domestic product". Our World in Data (2025). Data adapted from United Nations Industrial Development Organization. Retrieved from https://ourworldindata.org/grapher/total-manufacturing-value-added-from-high-tech [online resource]
[168] International Telecommunication Union – processed by Our World in Data. "2G network" [dataset]. International Telecommunication Union, "Data from multiple sources" [original data].
[169] World Bank – processed by Our World in Data. "Growth rate among the total population" [dataset]. World Bank
[170] "Data Page: Share of population below 50% of median income or consumption", part of the following publication: Joe Hasell, Max Roser, Esteban Ortiz-Ospina and Pablo Arriagada (2022) - "Poverty". Data adapted from World Bank Poverty and Inequality Platform. Retrieved from https://ourworldindata.org/grapher/relative-poverty-share-of-people-below-50-of-the-median [online resource]
[171] "Data Page: Share of adults reporting having felt discriminated against". Our World in Data (2025). Data adapted from Office of the United Nations High Commissioner for Human Rights. Retrieved from https://ourworldindata.org/grapher/share-of-the-population-reporting-having-felt-discriminated-against [online resource]
[172] International Labour Organisation – processed by Our World in Data. "10.4.1 - Labour share of GDP (%) - SL_EMP_GTOTL" [dataset]. International Labour Organisation [original data].
[173] World Bank – processed by Our World in Data. "After tax" [dataset]. World Bank, "World Bank (Collection agencies specified in footnote)" [original data].
[174] "Data Page: Migrant recruitment costs". Our World in Data (2025). Data adapted from International Labour Organization and World Bank. Retrieved from https://ourworldindata.org/grapher/migrant-recruitment-costs
[175] "Data Page: Proportion of countries with migration policies that facilitate orderly, safe, regular and responsible migration and mobility of people". Our World in Data (2025). Data adapted from International Organization for Migration, United Nations Department of Economic and Social Affairs and OECD as partner agency. Retrieved from https://ourworldindata.org/grapher/proportion-countries-migration-policies-criteria [online resource]
[176] "Data Page: Recorded deaths and disappearances during migration". Our World in Data (2025). Data adapted from International Organization for Migration. Retrieved from https://ourworldindata.org/grapher/deaths-and-disappearances-during-migration [online resource]
[177] UNHCR. (2024, October 8). *Refugee Data Finder - Key Indicators*. UNHCR. Retrieved January 27, 2025, from https://www.unhcr.org/refugee-statistics
[178] "Data Page: Share of products from least-developed countries that have no tariff". Our World in Data (2025). Data adapted from UN Conference on Trade and Development and World Trade Organisation. Retrieved from https://ourworldindata.org/grapher/proportion-tariff-lines-applied-to-imports-from-ldcs [online resource]
[179] Organisation for Economic Co-operation and Development – processed by Our World in Data. "10.b.1 - Total assistance for development, by recipient countries (millions of current United States dollars) - DC_TRF_TOTL" [dataset]. Organisation for Economic Co-operation and Development [original data].
[180] "Data Page: Official and private flows by donor", part of the following publication: Bastian Herre and Pablo Arriagada (2024) - "Foreign Aid". Data adapted from OECD. Retrieved from https://ourworldindata.org/grapher/foreign-aid-and-investments-given [online resource]
[181] World Bank – processed by Our World in Data. "10.c.1 - Average remittance costs of sending $200 for a sending country as a proportion of the amount remitted (%) - SI_RMT_COST_SND" [dataset]. World Bank [original data].
[182] UN. (2015). *United Nations Millennium Development Goals*. Retrieved January 27, 2025, from https://www.un.org/millenniumgoals/poverty.shtml
[183] UN-Habitat. (2020, February 7). The Participatory Slum Upgrading Programme (PSUP). UN-Habitat. Retrieved January 27, 2025, from https://unhabitat.org/programme/the-participatory-slum-upgrading-programme-psup
[184] "Data Page: Share of the urban population living in slums". Our World in Data (2025). Data adapted from United Nations Human Settlements Programme. Retrieved from https://ourworldindata.org/grapher/share-of-urban-population-living-in-slums [online resource]
[185] "Data Page: Share of urban populations with convenient access to public transport", part of the following publication: Hannah Ritchie, Veronika Samborska and Max Roser (2024) - "Urbanization". Data adapted from United Nations (2023). Retrieved from https://ourworldindata.org/grapher/share-with-convenient-access-to-public-transport [online resource]

[186] "Data Page: Cultural and natural heritage expenditure per capita". Our World in Data (2025). Data adapted from UNESCO Institute for Statistics. Retrieved from https://ourworldindata.org/grapher/expenditure-on-cultural-and-natural-heritage-per-capita [online resource]
[187] "Data Page: People affected by natural disasters", part of the following publication: Hannah Ritchie, Pablo Rosado and Max Roser (2022) - "Natural Disasters". Data adapted from EM-DAT, CRED / UCLouvain. Retrieved from https://ourworldindata.org/grapher/total-affected-by-natural-disasters [online resource]
[188] "Data Page: People left homeless from natural disasters", part of the following publication: Hannah Ritchie, Pablo Rosado and Max Roser (2022) - "Natural Disasters". Data adapted from EM-DAT, CRED / UCLouvain. Retrieved from https://ourworldindata.org/grapher/number-homeless-from-natural-disasters [online resource]
[189] Our World in Data based on EM-DAT, CRED / UCLouvain, Brussels, Belgium – www.emdat.be (D. Guha-Sapir) – processed by Our World in Data. "Death rates from disasters" [dataset]. Our World in Data based on EM-DAT, CRED / UCLouvain, Brussels, Belgium – www.emdat.be (D. Guha-Sapir) [original data].
[190] "Data Page: Global injuries from natural disasters", part of the following publication: Hannah Ritchie, Pablo Rosado and Max Roser (2022) - "Natural Disasters". Data adapted from EM-DAT, CRED / UCLouvain. Retrieved from https://ourworldindata.org/grapher/number-injured-from-disasters [online resource]
[191] Our World in Data based on EM-DAT, CRED / UCLouvain, Brussels, Belgium – www.emdat.be (D. Guha-Sapir) – processed by Our World in Data. "Number of deaths from disasters" [dataset]. Our World in Data based on EM-DAT, CRED / UCLouvain, Brussels, Belgium – www.emdat.be (D. Guha-Sapir) [original data].
[192] "Data Page: People displaced internally by natural disasters". Our World in Data (2025). Data adapted from Internal Displacement Monitoring Centre (via World Bank). Retrieved from https://ourworldindata.org/grapher/internally-displaced-persons-from-disasters [online resource]
[193] Our World in Data based on EM-DAT, CRED / UCLouvain, Brussels, Belgium – www.emdat.be (D. Guha-Sapir) – processed by Our World in Data
[194] Our World in Data based on EM-DAT, CRED / UCLouvain, Brussels, Belgium – www.emdat.be (D. Guha-Sapir) – processed by Our World in Data. "Total economic damages from disasters as a share of GDP" [dataset]. Our World in Data based on EM-DAT, CRED / UCLouvain, Brussels, Belgium – www.emdat.be (D. Guha-Sapir) [original data].
[195] "Data Page: Exposure to particulate matter air pollution". Our World in Data (2025). Data adapted from World Health Organization. Retrieved from https://ourworldindata.org/grapher/pm25-air-pollution [online resource]
[196] "Data Page: Urban policies that respond to population dynamics". Our World in Data (2025). Data adapted from United Nations Human Settlement Programme. Retrieved from https://ourworldindata.org/grapher/urban-policies-population-dynamics [online resource]
[197] "Data Page: Countries with a sustainable consumption and production national action plan". Our World in Data (2025). Data adapted from United Nations Environment Programme. Retrieved from https://ourworldindata.org/grapher/country-scp-plan [online resource]
[198] "Data Page: Domestic material consumption per capita". Our World in Data (2025). Data adapted from United Nations Environment Programme. Retrieved from https://ourworldindata.org/grapher/domestic-material-consumption-per-capita [online resource]; "Data Page: Material footprint per gross domestic product". Our World in Data (2025). Data adapted from United Nations Environment Programme. Retrieved from https://ourworldindata.org/grapher/material-footprint-per-unit-of-gdp [online resource]
[199] "Data Page: Food loss index". Our World in Data (2025). Data adapted from Food and Agriculture Organization of the United Nations. Retrieved from https://ourworldindata.org/grapher/global-food-loss-index [online resource]
[200] United Nations Environment Programme – processed by Our World in Data. "Basel Convention, Montreal Protocol, Rotterdam Convention, Stockholm Convention" [dataset]. United Nations Environment Programme, "Environment Live"
[201] "Data Page: Hazardous waste generated per capita". Our World in Data (2025). Data adapted from United Nations Environment Programme, United Nations Statistics Division and the United Nations Institute for Training and Research. Retrieved from https://ourworldindata.org/grapher/hazardous-waste-generated-per-capita [online resource]
[202] "Data Page: Municipal waste recycled". Our World in Data (2025). Data adapted from United Nations Environment Programme, United Nations Statistics Division and the United Nations Institute for Training and Research. Retrieved from https://ourworldindata.org/grapher/municipal-waste-recycled [online resource]
[203] "Data Page: Number of companies publishing sustainability reports that meet the minimum reporting requirements". Our World in Data (2025). Data adapted from United Nations Environment Programme and United Nations Conference on Trade and Development. Retrieved from https://ourworldindata.org/grapher/companies-publishing-sustainability-reports-minimum-requirements [online resource]
[204] "Data Page: Number of companies publishing sustainability reports that meet the minimum reporting requirements". Our World in Data (2025). Data adapted from United Nations Environment Programme and United Nations Conference on Trade and Development. Retrieved from https://ourworldindata.org/grapher/companies-publishing-sustainability-reports-minimum-requirements [online resource]
[205] UNEP. (2025). *Sustainable Public Procurement*. UNEP. Retrieved January 27, 2025, from https://www.unep.org/explore-topics/resource-efficiency/what-we-do/sustainable-public-procurement
[206] "Data Page: Level of implementation of sustainable procurement policies and plans". Our World in Data (2025). Data adapted from United Nations Environment Programme. Retrieved from https://ourworldindata.org/grapher/medium-high-level-implementation-of-sustainable-public-procurement [online resource]
[207] "Data Page: Renewable electricity-generating capacity per person". Our World in Data (2025). Data adapted from International Renewable Energy Agency and United Nations World Population Prospects. Retrieved from https://ourworldindata.org/grapher/renewable-electricity-generating-capacity-per-capita [online resource]
[208] "Data Page: Monitoring of sustainable tourism", part of the following publication: Bastian Herre and Veronika Samborska (2023) - "Tourism". Data adapted from UNWTO. Retrieved from https://ourworldindata.org/grapher/implementation-of-tools-to-monitor-economic-and-environmental-tourism
[209] Data from multiple sources compiled by the UN – processed by Our World in Data. "12.c.1 - Fossil-fuel subsidies (consumption and production) as a proportion of total GDP (%) - ER_FFS_CMPT_GDP" [dataset]. Data from multiple sources compiled by the UN [original data].
[210] Data from multiple sources compiled by the UN – processed by Our World in Data. "12.c.1 - Fossil-fuel subsidies (consumption and production) as a proportion of total GDP (%) - ER_FFS_CMPT_GDP" [dataset]. Data from multiple sources compiled by the UN [original data].

[211] Data from multiple sources compiled by the UN – processed by Our World in Data. "12.c.1 - Fossil-fuel subsidies (consumption and production) per capita (nominal United States dollars) - ER_FFS_CMPT_PC_CD" [dataset]. Data from multiple sources compiled by the UN [original data].

[212] Data from multiple sources compiled by the UN – processed by Our World in Data. "12.c.1 - Fossil-fuel subsidies (consumption and production) per capita (nominal United States dollars) - ER_FFS_CMPT_PC_CD" [dataset]. Data from multiple sources compiled by the UN [original data].

[213] "Data Page: Fossil-fuel subsidies". Our World in Data (2025). Data adapted from United Nations Environment Programme. Retrieved from https://ourworldindata.org/grapher/fossil-fuel-subsidies [online resource]

[214] "Data Page: Annual greenhouse gas emissions including land use", part of the following publication: Hannah Ritchie, Pablo Rosado and Max Roser (2023) - "CO_2 and Greenhouse Gas Emissions". Data adapted from Jones et al. Retrieved from https://ourworldindata.org/grapher/total-ghg-emissions [online resource]

[215] Jones et al. (2024) – with major processing by Our World in Data. "Annual greenhouse gas emissions including land use" [dataset]. Jones et al., "National contributions to climate change 2024.2" [original data]. Retrieved January 27, 2025, from https://ourworldindata.org/grapher/total-ghg-emissions

[216] "Data Page: Financial support provided through the Green Climate Fund". Our World in Data (2025). Data adapted from Data from multiple sources compiled by the UN. Retrieved from https://ourworldindata.org/grapher/green-climate-gcf-fund-pledges [online resource]

[217] "Data Page: Countries with national adaptation plans for climate change". Our World in Data (2025). Data adapted from UN Framework Convention on Climate Change. Retrieved from https://ourworldindata.org/grapher/countries-with-national-adaptation-plans-for-climate-change [online resource]

[218] "Data Page: Chlorophyll-a deviation from the global average". Our World in Data (2025). Data adapted from UN Statistics Division. Retrieved from https://ourworldindata.org/grapher/chlorophyll-a-deviation-from-the-global-average

[219] "Data Page: Beach litter". Our World in Data (2025). Data adapted from United Nations Environment Programme. Retrieved from https://ourworldindata.org/grapher/beach-litter [online resource]

[220] University of Hawaii – processed by Our World in Data. "Annual average" [dataset]. University of Hawaii [original data].

[221] "Data Page: Share of fish stocks within sustainable levels". Our World in Data (2025). Data adapted from Food and Agriculture Organization of the United Nations. Retrieved from https://ourworldindata.org/grapher/share-of-fish-stocks-that-are-sustainably-fished [online resource]

[222] "Data Page: Share of fish stocks within sustainable levels". Our World in Data (2025). Data adapted from Food and Agriculture Organization of the United Nations. Retrieved from https://ourworldindata.org/grapher/share-of-fish-stocks-that-are-sustainably-fished [online resource]

[223] "Data Page: Share of marine territorial waters that are protected". Our World in Data (2025). Data adapted from UN Environment Programme (via World Bank). Retrieved from https://ourworldindata.org/grapher/marine-protected-areas

[224] "Data Page: Protected area coverage of marine key biodiversity areas". Our World in Data (2025). Data adapted from BirdLife International, IUCN and UNEP-WCMC. Retrieved from https://ourworldindata.org/grapher/protected-area-coverage-of-marine-key-biodiversity-areas [online resource]

[225] "Data Page: Combatting illegal fishing". Our World in Data (2025). Data adapted from Food and Agriculture Organization of the United Nations. Retrieved from https://ourworldindata.org/grapher/regulation-illegal-fishing

[226] Food and Agriculture Organization. (2025). *14.4.1 Fish stocks sustainability | SDG Indicators Data Portal*. Retrieved January 27, 2025, from https://www.fao.org/sustainable-development-goals-data-portal/data/indicators/1441-fish-stocks-sustainability/en

[227] "Data Page: Sustainable fisheries as a proportion of gross domestic product". Our World in Data (2025). Data adapted from Food and Agriculture Organization of the United Nations. Retrieved from https://ourworldindata.org/grapher/sustainable-fisheries-as-a-proportion-of-gdp [online resource]

[228] "Data Page: Ocean science and research funding". Our World in Data (2025). Data adapted from Intergovernmental Oceanographic Commission of UNESCO. Retrieved from https://ourworldindata.org/grapher/ocean-research-funding

[229] "Data Page: Protection of the rights of small-scale fisheries". Our World in Data (2025). Data adapted from Data from multiple sources compiled by the UN. Retrieved from https://ourworldindata.org/grapher/protection-of-the-rights-of-small-scale-fisheries [online resource]

[230] Protected Planet. (2025). *Explore the World's Protected Areas*. Retrieved January 27, 2025, from https://www.protectedplanet.net/

[231] UN Food and Agriculture Organization (FAO). Forest Resources Assessment. – processed by Our World in Data. "Share of land area covered by forest" [dataset]. UN Food and Agriculture Organization (FAO). Forest Resources Assessment. [original data].

[232] UN Food and Agriculture Organization (FAO). Forest Resources Assessment. – processed by Our World in Data. "Share of land area covered by forest" [dataset]. UN Food and Agriculture Organization (FAO). Forest Resources Assessment. [original data].

[233] "Data Page: Share of land area that is protected". Our World in Data (2025). Data adapted from UN Environment Programme (via World Bank). Retrieved from https://ourworldindata.org/grapher/terrestrial-protected-areas

[234] "Data Page: Share of land area that is protected". Our World in Data (2025). Data adapted from UN Environment Programme (via World Bank). Retrieved from https://ourworldindata.org/grapher/terrestrial-protected-areas

[235] "Data Page: Share of terrestrial Key Biodiversity Areas that are protected". Our World in Data (2025). Data adapted from BirdLife International, IUCN and UNEP-WCMC. Retrieved from https://ourworldindata.org/grapher/protected-terrestrial-biodiversity-sites [online resource]

[236] "Data Page: Share of terrestrial Key Biodiversity Areas that are protected". Our World in Data (2025). Data adapted from BirdLife International, IUCN and UNEP-WCMC. Retrieved from https://ourworldindata.org/grapher/protected-terrestrial-biodiversity-sites [online resource]

[237] "Data Page: Annual change in forest area". Our World in Data (2025). Data adapted from Food and Agriculture Organization of the United Nations. Retrieved from https://ourworldindata.org/grapher/forest-area-net-change-rate

[238] "Data Page: Above-ground forest biomass". Our World in Data (2025). Data adapted from Food and Agriculture Organization of the United Nations. Retrieved from https://ourworldindata.org/grapher/above-ground-biomass-in-forest-per-hectare [online resource]

[239] "Data Page: Share of forest area within protected areas". Our World in Data (2025). Data adapted from Food and Agriculture Organization of the United Nations. Retrieved from https://ourworldindata.org/grapher/proportion-of-forest-area-within-legally-established-protected-areas [online resource]
[240] "Data Page: Share of forest with a long-term management plan". Our World in Data (2025). Data adapted from Food and Agriculture Organization of the United Nations. Retrieved from https://ourworldindata.org/grapher/proportion-of-forest-area-with-long-term-management-plan [online resource]
[241] "Data Page: Forest certified for sustainable use". Our World in Data (2025). Data adapted from Food and Agriculture Organization of the United Nations. Retrieved from https://ourworldindata.org/grapher/proportion-of-forest-area-certified-under-an-independently-verified-certification-scheme [online resource]
[242] "Data Page: Share of land that is degraded". Our World in Data (2025). Data adapted from United Nations Convention to Combat Desertification. Retrieved from https://ourworldindata.org/grapher/share-degraded-land [online resource]
[243] "Data Page: Red List Index". Our World in Data (2025). Data adapted from BirdLife International and IUCN. Retrieved from https://ourworldindata.org/grapher/red-list-index
[244] "Data Page: Countries using the System of Environmental-Economic Accounting". Our World in Data (2025). Data adapted from United Nations Environment Programme, Convention on Biological Diversity and United Nations Statistics Division. Retrieved from https://ourworldindata.org/grapher/countries-using-the-system-of-environmental-economic-accounting [online resource]
[245] "Data Page: Total donations received for biodiversity conservation". Our World in Data (2025). Data adapted from Organisation for Economic Co-operation and Development. Retrieved from https://ourworldindata.org/grapher/total-oda-for-biodiversity-by-recipient [online resource]
[246] "Data Page: Homicide rate", part of the following publication: Bastian Herre, Fiona Spooner and Max Roser (2013) - "Homicides". Data adapted from United Nations Office on Drugs and Crime, Various sources. Retrieved from https://ourworldindata.org/grapher/homicide-rate-unodc [online resource]
[247] "Data Page: Homicide rate", part of the following publication: Bastian Herre, Fiona Spooner and Max Roser (2013) - "Homicides". Data adapted from United Nations Office on Drugs and Crime, Various sources. Retrieved from https://ourworldindata.org/grapher/homicide-rate-unodc [online resource]
[248] "Data Page: Deaths in armed conflicts based on where they occurred", part of the following publication: Bastian Herre, Lucas Rodés-Guirao and Max Roser (2024) - "War and Peace". Data adapted from Uppsala Conflict Data Program, Natural Earth. Retrieved from https://ourworldindata.org/grapher/deaths-in-armed-conflicts-by-country [online resource]
[249] "Data Page: Share of children who experienced violence". Our World in Data (2025). Data adapted from UNICEF. Retrieved from https://ourworldindata.org/grapher/share-of-children-who-experienced-violence [online resource]
[250] "Data Page: Human trafficking victims". Our World in Data (2025). Data adapted from UN Office on Drugs and Crime. Retrieved from https://ourworldindata.org/grapher/human-trafficking-victims [online resource]
[251] UN Office on Drugs and Crime – processed by Our World in Data. "Boys" [dataset]. UN Office on Drugs and Crime, "GLOTIP Database" [original data].
[252] UN Office on Drugs and Crime – processed by Our World in Data. "Men" [dataset]. UN Office on Drugs and Crime, "GLOTIP Database" [original data].
[253] "Data Page: Share of young women who experienced sexual violence as children". Our World in Data (2025). Data adapted from UNICEF. Retrieved from https://ourworldindata.org/grapher/women-who-experienced-sexual-violence-by-age-18 [online resource]
[254] "Data Page: Unsentenced detainees as a proportion of overall prison population". Our World in Data (2025). Data adapted from United Nations Office on Drugs and Crime. Retrieved from https://ourworldindata.org/grapher/unsentenced-detainees-as-proportion-of-prison-population [online resource]
[255] "Data Page: Bribery prevalence". Our World in Data (2025). Data adapted from United Nations Office on Drugs and Crime. Retrieved from https://ourworldindata.org/grapher/bribery-prevalence-un [online resource]
[256] "Data Page: Bribery incidence for firms". Our World in Data (2025). Data adapted from World Bank. Retrieved from https://ourworldindata.org/grapher/bribery-incidence-for-firms [online resource]
[257] "Data Page: Representation of women in the judiciary". Our World in Data (2025). Data adapted from Inter-Parliamentary Union. Retrieved from https://ourworldindata.org/grapher/representation-of-women-in-the-judiciary
[258] "Data Page: Share of population satisfied with government services". Our World in Data (2025). Data adapted from United Nations Development Programme. Retrieved from https://ourworldindata.org/grapher/share-of-population-satisfied-with-government-services [online resource]
[259] "Data Page: Lower chamber female legislators", part of the following publication: Bastian Herre, Lucas Rodés-Guirao and Esteban Ortiz-Ospina (2013) - "Democracy". Data adapted from V-Dem. Retrieved from https://ourworldindata.org/grapher/share-of-women-in-parliament [online resource]
[260] "Data Page: Representation of women in the judiciary". Our World in Data (2025). Data adapted from Inter-Parliamentary Union. Retrieved from https://ourworldindata.org/grapher/representation-of-women-in-the-judiciary
[261] "Data Page: Share of births registered". Our World in Data (2025). Data adapted from UNICEF. Retrieved from https://ourworldindata.org/grapher/births-registered [online resource]
[262] Office of the United Nations High Commissioner for Human Rights – processed by Our World in Data. "Female" [dataset]. Office of the United Nations High Commissioner for Human Rights, "OHCHR" [original data].
[263] "Data Page: Countries with policy guarantees for public access to information". Our World in Data (2025). Data adapted from UNESCO. Retrieved from https://ourworldindata.org/grapher/countries-that-adopt-guarantees-for-public-access-to-information [online resource]
[264] "Data Page: Share of countries with accredited independent national human rights institutions". Our World in Data (2025). Data adapted from United Nations High Commissioner for Human Rights and Global Alliance of National Human Rights Institutions. Retrieved from https://ourworldindata.org/grapher/share-countries-accredited-independent-national-human-rights-institutions [online resource]
[265] "Data Page: Share of adults reporting having felt discriminated against". Our World in Data (2025). Data adapted from Office of the United Nations High Commissioner for Human Rights. Retrieved from https://ourworldindata.org/grapher/share-of-the-population-reporting-having-felt-discriminated-against [online resource]
[266] "Data Page: Government revenues as a share of GDP". Our World in Data (2025). Data adapted from International Monetary Fund. Retrieved from https://ourworldindata.org/grapher/government-revenues-as-a-share-of-gdp-imf

[267] "Data Page: Share of central government expenditures funded by taxes". Our World in Data (2025). Data adapted from International Monetary Fund. Retrieved from https://ourworldindata.org/grapher/share-of-central-government-expenditures-funded-by-taxes [online resource]

[268] "Data Page: Foreign aid given as a share of national income", part of the following publication: Bastian Herre and Pablo Arriagada (2024) - "Foreign Aid". Data adapted from OECD. Retrieved from https://ourworldindata.org/grapher/foreign-aid-given-as-a-share-of-national-income-net [online resource]

[269] "Data Page: Foreign aid given to least-developed countries as a share of donor's national income". Our World in Data (2025). Data adapted from Organisation for Economic Co-operation and Development. Retrieved from https://ourworldindata.org/grapher/foreign-aid-given-to-least-developed-countries-as-a-share-of-donors-national-income

[270] "Data Page: Foreign direct investment, net inflows as share of GDP". Our World in Data (2025). Data adapted from Data compiled from multiple sources by World Bank. Retrieved from https://ourworldindata.org/grapher/foreign-direct-investment-net-inflows-as-share-of-gdp [online resource]

[271] "Data Page: Foreign direct investment, net inflows as share of GDP". Our World in Data (2025). Data adapted from Data compiled from multiple sources by World Bank. Retrieved from https://ourworldindata.org/grapher/foreign-direct-investment-net-inflows-as-share-of-gdp [online resource]

[272] "Data Page: Debt service as a share of exports of good and services". Our World in Data (2025). Data adapted from World Bank. Retrieved from https://ourworldindata.org/grapher/debt-service-of-exports-of-goods-services [online resource]

[273] Zhan JX, Santos-Paulino AU. Investing in the Sustainable Development Goals: Mobilization, channeling, and impact. J Int Bus Policy. 2021;4(1):166–83. doi: 10.1057/s42214-020-00093-3. Epub 2021 Feb 8. PMCID: PMC7868860.

[274] UN Conference on Trade and Development – processed by Our World in Data. "17.5.1 - Number of countries with a signed bilateral investment treaty (BIT) with least developed countries and developing countries (Number) - SG_CPA_SIGN_BIT" [dataset]. UN Conference on Trade and Development [original data].

[275] "Data Page: Landline Internet subscriptions per 100 people". Our World in Data (2025). Data adapted from International Telecommunication Union (via World Bank). Retrieved from https://ourworldindata.org/grapher/broadband-penetration-by-country [online resource]

[276] "Data Page: Export of environmentally sound technologies". Our World in Data (2025). Data adapted from UN Statistics Division. Retrieved from https://ourworldindata.org/grapher/export-of-environmentally-sound-technologies

[277] "Data Page: Share of the population using the Internet", part of the following publication: Hannah Ritchie, Edouard Mathieu, Max Roser and Esteban Ortiz-Ospina (2023) - "Internet". Data adapted from World Bank. Retrieved from https://ourworldindata.org/grapher/share-of-individuals-using-the-internet [online resource]

[278] "Data Page: Total official development assistance for technical co-operation". Our World in Data (2025). Data adapted from Organisation for Economic Co-operation and Development. Retrieved from https://ourworldindata.org/grapher/total-official-development-assistance-for-technical-cooperation [online resource]

[279] "Data Page: Tariff rate across all products". Our World in Data (2025). Data adapted from World Bank based on data from the World Integrated Trade Solution platform. Retrieved from https://ourworldindata.org/grapher/tariff-rate-applied-weighted-mean-all-products [online resource]

[280] "Data Page: Share of global merchandise exports". Our World in Data (2025). Data adapted from UN Conference on Trade and Development and World Trade Organization. Retrieved from https://ourworldindata.org/grapher/share-of-global-merchandise-exports [online resource]

[281] Multiple sources compiled by World Bank (2024) – processed by Our World in Data. "All products" [dataset]. World Bank based on data from the World Integrated Trade Solution platform, "World Development Indicators" [original data].

[282] "Data Page: Inflation of consumer prices". Our World in Data (2025). Data adapted from International Monetary Fund (via World Bank). Retrieved from https://ourworldindata.org/grapher/inflation-of-consumer-prices [online resource]

[283] "Data Page: Gross public sector debt as a share of gross domestic product". Our World in Data (2025). Data adapted from World Bank. Retrieved from https://ourworldindata.org/grapher/gross-public-sector-debt-as-a-proportion-of-gdp

[284] "Data Page: Mechanisms in place to enhance policy coherence for sustainable development". Our World in Data (2025). Data adapted from United Nations Environment Programme. Retrieved from https://ourworldindata.org/grapher/mechanisms-to-enhance-policy-for-sustainable-development [online resource]

[285] OECD and United Nations Development Programme – processed by Our World in Data. "17.15.1 - Proportion of results indicators drawn from country-led results frameworks - data by recipient (%) - SG_PLN_RECRICTRY" [dataset]. OECD and United Nations Development Programme, "OECD and UNDP." [original data].

[286] OECD and UN Development Programme – processed by Our World in Data. "Providers" [dataset]. OECD and UN Development Programme, "Organisation for Economic Co-operation and Development (OECD) and United Nations Development Programme (UNDP)." [original data].

[287] "Data Page: Money committed to public-private partnerships for infrastructure". Our World in Data (2025). Data adapted from World Bank. Retrieved from https://ourworldindata.org/grapher/money-committed-to-public-private-partnerships-for-infrastructure [online resource]

[288] 288 World Data Lab. (2024). World Poverty Clock. Retrieved December 2024, from https://worldpoverty.io/

[289] "Data Page: Countries with statistical legislation in line with UN Fundamental Principles of Official Statistics". Our World in Data (2025). Data adapted from PARIS21 SDG Survey. Retrieved from https://ourworldindata.org/grapher/national-statistical-legislation [online resource]

[290] Data from multiple sources compiled by the UN – processed by Our World in Data. "17.19.1 - Dollar value of all resources made available to strengthen statistical capacity in developing countries (current United States dollars) - SG_STT_CAPTY" [dataset]. Data from multiple sources compiled by the UN [original data]; Data from multiple sources compiled by the UN – processed by Our World in Data. "17.19.1 - Dollar value of all resources made available to strengthen statistical capacity in developing countries (current United States dollars) - SG_STT_CAPTY" [dataset]. Data from multiple sources compiled by the UN [original data].

[291] "Data Page: Population census recently completed", part of the following publication: Bastian Herre and Pablo Arriagada (2023) - "State Capacity". Data adapted from UN Statistics Division. Retrieved from https://ourworldindata.org/grapher/population-census-world-bank [online resource]

[292] "Data Page: Share of deaths that are registered", part of the following publication: Hannah Ritchie, Lucas Rodés-Guirao, Edouard Mathieu, Marcel Gerber, Esteban Ortiz-Ospina, Joe Hasell and Max Roser (2023) - "Population Growth". Data adapted from Ariel Karlinsky. Retrieved from https://ourworldindata.org/grapher/share-of-deaths-registered [online resource]

www.ingramcontent.com/pod-product-compliance
Lightning Source LLC
LaVergne TN
LVHW021947060526
838200LV00043B/1947